********** UN **********
FK
UPABLE

50 Recipes That Even You Can't Screw Up

ZACH GOLDEN

RUNNING PRESS
PHILADELPHIA

Running Press
Hachette Book Group
1290 Avenue of the Americas, New York, NY 10104
www.runningpress.com
@Running_Press

Printed in China

First Edition: October 2020

Published by Running Press, an imprint of Perseus Books, LLC, a subsidiary of Hachette Book Group, Inc. The Running Press name and logo is a trademark of the Hachette Book Group.

The Hachette Speakers Bureau provides a wide range of authors for speaking events. To find out more, go to www.hachettespeakersbureau.com or call (866) 376-6591.

The publisher is not responsible for websites (or their content) that are not owned by the publisher.

Print book cover and interior design by Rachel Peckman.

Library of Congress Control Number: 2020937388

ISBNs: 978-0-7624-9957-1 (hardcover), 978-0-7624-9958-8 (ebook)

10 9 8 7 6 5 4 3 2 1

For Sara, Oscar, and Teddy, but mostly the Buffalo Bills

Contents

Let's not fuck stuff up, together

If you are reading this, it's more than likely you are not a good cook. But that's okay, because I am a good cook, and together we're somewhere between passable and good.

Unfuckupable food is fast, delicious, and, most of all, easy. The recipes in this book use simple techniques and easy-to-find ingredients and were created under the assumption that you are completely impotent in the kitchen and most likely in other areas of your life as well.

Every recipe in this book was tested for unfuckupability by novice cooks, small children, and New England Patriots fans, who are notoriously unintelligent. They didn't fuck up any of the dishes, and you won't either if you just follow the . . .

FIVE RULES OF UNFUCKUPABILITY

Rule 1:
Good ingredients taste good; bad ingredients taste bad

If you cook with ingredients that taste good on their own, it's really hard to fuck them up, so try to find fresh, seasonal, local ingredients whenever possible. Go to a farmers' market or join a CSA. Grow it yourself. Steal from a Whole Foods—Jeff Bezos can afford it. Good ingredients make cooking easier, and you need all the help you can get, so don't settle for bad.

Rule 2:
Unfuckitup in prep

Avoid surprises like you have a deep-seated, pathological fear of them. Surprises are your enemy now. Surprises taste like shit, so to avoid them, you're going to:

* Read the entire recipe before starting a dish. Don't find out that you're doomed 30 minutes in. We don't waste food in this house. What am I, made of money?

* Make sure you have all the necessary ingredients for the recipe. If you don't, find either a suitable substitute or a different recipe.

* Do all the prep work before you start cooking. Put ingredients in little bowls, and keep your space clean and organized. When shit hits the fan, and it will, you'll be ready-ish.

Rule 3:
Fucking google it

You have the entirety of human knowledge at your fingertips, so if there's a technique you don't understand, an ingredient you need to find a substitute for, or you just need some encouragement, just fucking google it. Or AskJeeves, either way.

Rule 4:
Fuck your heart

Salt is what makes food delicious. If you ever taste something and you're like, "It needs something," that something is almost definitely salt, and even if it's not, salt will probably still fix it. The reason restaurant food tastes better than your food is because they use an ungodly amount of salt—also they don't suck at cooking. If you don't trust me, trust them: salt your damn food.

Salty is subjective. I haven't included measurements for salt and pepper in these recipes, with a few exceptions. Instead, I'll forcefully tell you when to season the dishes and leave the amount up to you so that you can season to your taste. Remember, you can always add more salt, but removing salt is considerably more difficult without access to time travel. So go easy, taste it, then adjust, and repeat until it's delicious or you have a massive heart attack.

Rule 5: Taste your fucking food

Taste everything while cooking, and trust your taste buds. If it tastes good, great; if it tastes bad, you probably made a mistake because I specifically wrote these recipes to be good-tasting. The amounts and ratios in these recipes are tested, tried, and true, but if you want or need to adjust them to suit your tastes, feel free, but just remember: if you fuck it up and it's awful, that's 100 percent on you, not me. I will tolerate no complaining.

Before you set off on your journey of unfuckupability, just remember one last thing:

YOU CAN DO IT! *

* hopefully

Hangover Breakfast Sandwich

The only hangover cure better than this sandwich is this sandwich and also smoking weed. It's greasy and salty and will probably chip a few weeks off your life expectancy, but you'll feel noticeably less shitty the moment it hits your bloodstream, especially if you smoked a whole bunch of the sticky icky first. Now, I'll admit—this isn't the easiest thing to make hungover and extremely morning-high. There are ample opportunities to cut yourself, burn yourself, and irreparably change your life for the worse. But it'll distract you from how shitty you feel, and there's a delicious reward at the end (assuming you live to see it), so it's worth the risk.

3 slices bacon	2 large eggs, beaten
A bunch of unsalted butter, divided	Honey
	Hot sauce
2 slices good bread or 1 English muffin	½ ripe avocado
1 slice American cheese	Kosher salt and freshly ground black pepper

First, cook the bacon in whatever way you want. An aluminum-foil-lined sheet pan in a 425°F oven for about 15 minutes does the trick. As does frying it in a skillet. As does the microwave, kinda. This part is up to you, unless you're not only bad at cooking but also pathologically indecisive, in which case do it in the oven: it's safest, unless you pass out and forget about it . . . Okay, you know what? Do it in the microwave.

Butter each slice of bread on both sides, using enough butter that your heart takes it personally.

Put a heavy griddle over medium heat and add the bread, cooking it until golden brown, 2 to 3 minutes per side. Flip the bread and add a slice of cheese to one slice and remove from the heat. The heat from the pan will melt the cheese while you make the eggs.

Heat unsalted butter in a nonstick pan over medium heat until it bubbles. Add the beaten eggs and season them with plenty of salt and pepper. Using a rubber spatula, pull the cooked edges of the eggs to the center and tilt the pan so that the runny part of the eggs recoats the edges. Continue to move the eggs around until they are no longer runny, about 2 minutes. Fold the eggs in half to make a half moon, then fold the half moon in half so that it's sandwich sized.

To assemble, top the cheesy toast with the eggs and add the bacon. Add a drizzle of honey and drown everything in however much hot sauce you can handle. Using a spoon, scoop the avocado from its skin and mash it into the top piece of toast. Reunite the two halves of toast, serve immediately, and feel your urge to aggressively vomit fade away.

Makes 1 sandwich

Hash Browns

McDonald's is the gold standard for hash browns. This recipe is not for McDonald's hash browns. If you want those, go to a McDonald's and they'll gladly make you one for one American dollar and save you the trouble. But if you want to make them yourself, keep in mind that a good hash brown should be salty, buttery, and, above all else, crispy. It's important to remember: one does not simply luck their way into crispy hash browns; it takes discipline and dedication, hard work, and scarring grease burns from trial and error. So any youths or millennials who think simply showing up and doing the bare minimum entitles them to crispiness— well, they've got a limp, flaccid disappointment in their future.

2 pounds russet potatoes, peeled	Freshly ground black pepper
Kosher salt	4 tablespoons unsalted butter
½ teaspoon garlic powder	4 tablespoons extra-virgin olive oil
½ teaspoon onion powder	

Shred the potatoes using either a food processor or the largest holes on a box grater, being very careful not to include small chunks of finger with the potato. Add the shredded potato to a colander and rinse under cold running water until the water draining from the potatoes runs clear.

Drain the potatoes and transfer them to a clean dishcloth. Wrap the potatoes in the dishcloth and hold it over the sink, twisting to wring out as much liquid as you can to preserve the all-important crisposity. Now do this two or three more times, because I'm not convinced you did a good enough job the first time. If you want that crunch, you gotta work for it.

Transfer the potatoes to a mixing bowl and toss with at least 1 teaspoon of salt (more if you want it to be delicious and aren't afraid of unplanned cardiac emergencies), the garlic and onion powder, and lots of freshly ground pepper.

Put a large heavy skillet over medium-high heat and add the butter and oil. Add the shredded potato mixture and distribute evenly. Cook for 5 minutes, until a deep golden crispy crust forms on the bottom; then either go full YOLO and try to flip the entire hash brown in one fell swoop and most likely fail or, using a rubber spatula, break up the hash brown into manageable pieces and flip those. Either way, cook until the outsides are crispy on both sides and look a heavenly golden brown, about 5 to 8 minutes more.

When the hash browns are properly crispy, remove from the pan and transfer to a plate lined with paper towels to drain. Season aggressively with salt. Don't worry; your heart will be fine. Crispiness is scientifically proven to ward off heart disease.

Serves 4

Apple Dutch Baby

When I was growing up, my mom made huge homemade Dutch babies for us on the weekends. They were my favorite breakfast or breakfast-for-dinner food, until one day she asked adorable, angelic, innocent child me to bring the heavy cast-iron skillet containing the Dutch baby to the table. Being a good boy, I hopped to, but when I grabbed the handle, my skin sizzled, and I suddenly smelled chicken. Much to my mom's horror, I tried to drop the skillet, but thankfully my hand stuck to the handle. She ran over, took her sweet time putting on oven mitts, and pried the handle from my hand. And in all the panic, through my screams of agony, and in the face of scars that decades later are luckily only emotional, she managed to not ruin the Dutch baby. So unless your child is having an emergency while making this, you don't really have any excuse.

3 large eggs
¾ cup whole milk
¾ cup all-purpose flour
2 teaspoons vanilla extract
Pinch of kosher salt
½ teaspoon ground ginger
¼ teaspoon ground cloves
¼ teaspoon ground nutmeg
1 teaspoon ground
 cinnamon, divided

4 tablespoons unsalted
 butter, divided
2 medium Honeycrisp or
 lesser apples, peeled and
 sliced ¼ inch thick
1 tablespoon light brown
 sugar
A shitload of real maple
 syrup

Preheat your oven to 425°F. In a blender or food processor, combine the eggs, milk, flour, vanilla, salt, ground ginger, ground cloves, ground nutmeg, and ½ teaspoon of the ground cinnamon and blend for 15 seconds. If you don't have a blender or food processor, use a mixing bowl and whisk like hell for 1 minute or until you can't stop complaining that your arm hurts. Set the batter aside to rest for at least 10 minutes.

Put a large heavy skillet over medium heat. Add 2 tablespoons of the butter. When it starts to bubble, add the sliced apple, brown sugar, and remaining ½ teaspoon of cinnamon. Sauté, stirring often, until the apple is caramely and soft, about 5 minutes. Transfer to a plate and reserve.

Wipe out the skillet or (if you're a bourgeois capitalist pig who owns multiple skillets while so much of the world would literally and gladly kill members of their own family for the dream of owning but one skillet) grab a clean skillet and put it in the preheated oven for at least 10 minutes to become skin-meltingly hot. If you skip this part, your Dutch baby will not rise, and even though it will still taste good, it will haunt you as you become obsessed, wondering about what could have been.

Remove the skillet from the oven and add the remaining 2 tablespoons of butter. Swirl the melted butter evenly around the bottom and sides, then add the cooked apples back to the skillet and pour the batter over them. Bake in the oven until the Dutch baby is puffed up and golden brown around the edges, about 12 to 15 minutes. Remove from the oven, let cool for 5 minutes, then serve immediately with fresh maple syrup, not the imitation stuff that for some reason my wife prefers and which will someday be the end of our marriage.

Serves 4

Eggs in Purgatory

The concepts of heaven and hell are genius in
their simplicity: be good and go to heaven; be bad
and go to hell. They taught countless millions
to live morally lest they suffer for eternity, and
they shot Catholicism into the upper echelons
of religions. But the Catholics got greedy and
overplayed their hand, introducing a third
destination: purgatory, a confusing pre-hell where
sinners remain until they enter heaven by atoning
for their sins or scoring an invite from a friend
who knows the doorman. Eggs in purgatory was
the Catholic Church's attempt to distract from
their mistake, to rebrand purgatory so that when
people hear it they think of delicious tender eggs
cooked in a spicy tomato-y sauce. Even though
I'm highly critical of the Catholic Church, you've
got to give credit where credit is due: they know
their eggs.

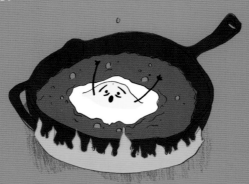

1/3 cup olive oil
8 garlic cloves, smashed
1 (28-ounce) can whole
  peeled tomatoes
1 teaspoon crushed red
  pepper flakes
1/2 teaspoon ground cumin
1/2 teaspoon sweet paprika
Kosher salt and freshly
  ground black pepper

1 bunch Tuscan kale leaves,
  destemmed and sliced
  into 1/2-inch ribbons
8 large eggs
1/3 cup chopped fresh
  cilantro
Crusty bread for sauce
  sopping

Put a large heavy skillet over medium heat and add the olive oil. Add the smashed garlic and sauté, stirring constantly so that the garlic doesn't burn, about 1 to 2 minutes. Add the tomatoes, red pepper flakes, cumin, and paprika and season with plenty of salt and pepper. Cover the skillet and cook for 10 minutes.

Use a wooden spoon to mash the tomatoes so that they break apart and release their juices until the mixture is saucy. Reduce the heat to medium-low and stir in the Tuscan kale leaves.

Crack the eggs one at a time into a small bowl. If you're unconcerned about choking, possibly to death, on large fragments of eggshell, go ahead and crack the eggs right into the skillet. Add the eggs to the skillet one at a time, spacing them evenly. Season the eggs aggressively with salt and pepper, then cover the pan and cook until the egg whites are set but yolks are still runny, about 5 minutes. Check to make sure your eggs are cooked so that you don't literally send whoever eats this to purgatory, then remove from the heat. Top with chopped cilantro and serve with some crusty bread for sopping up the sauce. Congratulations: you have now atoned for any culinary sins.

Serves 4

Pancetta, Arugula, and Mozzarella Frittata

I do the cooking at home because we're woke as fuck and breaking normative gender roles is kind of our thing, and also because my wife isn't a very good cook. She is, however, emetophobic, which means that she has a pathological fear of vomit, and in the ten-plus years we've been together, she's thrown up only once, but it just so happened to be three hours after I made her this dish for the first time. Things got tense. She accused me of food poisoning her, and despite my assurances that my frittata couldn't possibly be the culprit because the first symptoms of food poisoning typically present at least six hours after eating (God, read a book), and the fact that I ate the frittata and not only felt great but also felt like dancing, she decided it was my and the frittata's fault. I'd like to note for posterity's sake that I held back my wife's hair as she vomited, and later, when she was chastising me for causing this ordeal by lovingly making her a home-cooked meal, I reminded her of this, to which she snapped back, "It was only a strand!" And even if it was only a strand, that totally counts, and now hopefully you see the type of person I'm dealing with.

6 ounces arugula
2 garlic cloves, minced
2 tablespoons olive oil, divided
8 large eggs
¼ teaspoon crushed red pepper flakes

2 tablespoons grated Parmesan cheese
4 ounces pancetta, finely diced
4 ounces fresh mozzarella, thinly sliced
Kosher salt and freshly ground black pepper

Preheat your oven to 400°F. In a mixing bowl, combine the arugula, garlic, and 1 tablespoon of the olive oil. Toss the greens until coated, then season with salt and pepper. Taste and adjust the seasoning until it tastes good.

In a separate mixing bowl, crack the eggs and beat for 30 seconds, until smooth and fully incorporated—no gross globs allowed. Season with plenty of salt and pepper, then add the red pepper flakes and grated Parmesan cheese. If you'd like to add food poisoning to your dish, please do so now.

Put a large cast-iron or nonstick skillet over medium-high heat and add the remaining 1 tablespoon of olive oil. When the oil begins to smoke, add the pancetta to the pan and sauté until it starts to crisp up, about 2 minutes. Add the arugula mixture to the pan and cook until the greens start to wilt, stirring constantly, 1 minute more.

Reduce the heat to medium and pour the egg mixture into the skillet. Using a spatula, push the cooked outer edges to the middle and tilt the pan so that the raw egg coats the skillet evenly. Add the slices of mozzarella and cook for 3 minutes, occasionally running your spatula under the eggs so that they don't stick to the pan.

Transfer the skillet to the top rack of your oven and bake until the top of the frittata is cooked and the cheese is melted, about 8 to 10 minutes. Remove from the oven, let cool for at least 5 minutes, and serve it straight from the skillet, making sure to indemnify yourself from whatever happens after consumption.

Serves 4

Tortilla Española

I first tried this dish while traveling in Spain. It's a staple at tapas and pintxo bars as well as cafés around the country and is eaten for breakfast, lunch, and probably dinner too—I'm not sure: they eat at like 11:00 p.m. and I try to be asleep by 9:30. When I asked the chefs in Spain how they made their tortilla española, they rudely responded in Spanish, so I had to make it up because I only speak American and also a little French because I'm worldly. So while this might not be the most authentic way to do it, it tastes just as good and is probably easier, especially if you don't speak Spanish. Think of it as a tortilla for the non-española.

2 pounds potatoes, diced
½ cup olive oil
1 medium onion, thinly
  sliced
10 large eggs, beaten

½ cup chopped fresh
  parsley
Bread, for serving
Kosher salt and freshly
  ground black pepper

Preheat your oven to 400°F. Prep your ingredients. When dicing the potatoes, make sure they are all roughly the same size so that they cook evenly and aren't starchy and awful. Take your time, breathe, listen to Tony Robbins if you have to; you can probably do it.

Heat a large, heavy, ideally cast-iron pan over medium-high heat and add the olive oil. When the oil begins to smoke, add the potatoes very carefully, unless you want a souvenir of your meal in the form of a permanent scarring grease burn. Fry the potatoes, stirring occasionally, for 15 minutes. Add the onion and sauté until the potatoes are golden brown, about 5 to 10 minutes more. Taste one. If it's cooked through, it's ready; if it's not, cook for a few more minutes and then check again.

Turn the heat down to medium, season the potatoes with salt and freshly ground pepper, and scrape the pan to release any stuck-on bits. Taste a potato and adjust the seasoning as needed. Add the beaten eggs and chopped parsley and swirl to evenly distribute. Give the pan a scrape with a rubber spatula to make sure the eggs don't stick to the sides or bottom. Put the pan in the oven to bake for 10 minutes, then remove and let it cool for 5 minutes.

Getting the tortilla out of the pan is the hardest part of this dish, provided you didn't suffer a grease burn. You'll need to use a little bit of muscle to get it to release from the pan cleanly. Put a cutting board on the counter. Grab the pan with dishtowels or an oven mitt, and in one decisive motion flip the pan and BANG it down onto the cutting board. Then either slice the tortilla, serve with toasted bread, and enjoy, or pick up the tortilla that you spilled all over the floor and order takeout.

Serves 4

Southwestern Shrimp Salad

I live my life in strict adherence to the Taco Salad Theorem, which posits that the mere presence of lettuce in a dish is what constitutes a salad and that the more unhealthy things you put in to distract from how gross lettuce is, the better. This salad is full of healthy shit, but it doesn't taste like it because of spicy shrimps, cheese, avocado, and tortilla chips. This is not one of those get-hangry-two-hours-after-eating-and-"accidentally"-stab-someone-with-a-nail-clipper salads; it is a verifiable meal, and if you try this and disagree, you should probably eat smaller portions—we're all worried about you.

12 ounces raw shell-on shrimp, peeled and deveined, unless you don't mind eating shrimp ass
2 garlic cloves, thinly sliced
1 teaspoon chili flakes
2 tablespoons olive oil
1 ripe avocado, diced
4 to 6 scallions, thinly sliced, or to taste
6 radishes, thinly sliced
1 pound cherry tomatoes, halved
1 cup cooked black beans, rinsed and drained
Juice of 1 lime, divided
8 to 10 ounces romaine or mesclun mix lettuce
6 ounces pepper jack cheese, grated
Tortilla chips
Kosher salt and freshly ground black pepper

Get the shrimp marinating before you prep the other ingredients so that your salad doesn't get soggy and lackluster because you didn't have the wherewithal to plan ahead, despite being reminded a somewhat insulting number of times. In a mixing bowl, combine the shrimp, sliced garlic, chili flakes, and olive oil. Season it with a lot of salt and pepper. Cover and set aside.

Add the avocado, scallions, radishes, tomatoes, and beans to a large bowl. Squeeze half a lime into the bowl and season lightly with salt and pepper. Taste and adjust the seasoning until it tastes like a better cook made it.

Put a heavy skillet over medium-high heat. Put your hand about an inch from the skillet's surface. When it feels hot, it's ready. Add the shrimp and marinade into the skillet and cook for 2 minutes per side. Taste a shrimp; if it's gummy and gross, cook it for 1 additional minute then recheck it and repeat until not gross. If it's chewy and tough, you have overcooked the shrimp, and there is nothing you can do but pray and hope that whomever you're serving this to has an extremely unsophisticated palate. When it's properly cooked, remove from the heat, squeeze the other half of the lime into the skillet, and toss to coat.

Add the lettuce, cheese, and tortilla chips to the salad bowl and toss. Taste it and adjust the seasoning. If the lettuce tastes underdressed, add more lime juice; if it's overdressed, add more lettuce. Divide the salad into bowls and top with shrimp. Spoon some of the garlic and chili flake–infused oil from the pan atop each salad and serve immediately. Every second you wait, the salad gets soggier, so would it kill you to hustle?

Serves 4

"Caesar" Salad

Authenticity is overrated in food. I was once traveling through Provence when a local who I hope is dead right now told me that andouillette was an authentic local delicacy that I absolutely must try. What this person neglected to tell me was that andouillette smelled, tasted, and in fact quite literally was pig colon sausage stuffed with whatever the pig had in its ass prior to being murdered. Ever since that day, I have sworn off authenticity. While this isn't the most authentic Caesar salad in the world, it's easier than the real thing, it tastes great, and with your pedestrian palate, you probably won't be able to tell the difference. Also, most importantly, I guarantee you that there is no surprise pig colon in this recipe. You have my word.

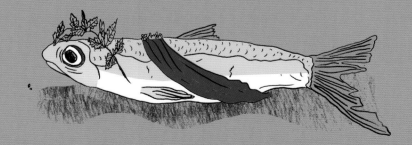

½ loaf crusty French bread, cut into 1-inch cubes
½ cup extra-virgin olive oil, divided
2 teaspoons garlic powder
1 garlic clove, finely minced
3 oil-packed anchovy fillets, roughly chopped
2 tablespoons Dijon mustard
½ teaspoon Worcestershire sauce
2 tablespoons fresh lemon juice
3 tablespoons mayonnaise
3 romaine hearts, chopped into 2-inch pieces
1 cup shredded Parmesan cheese
Kosher salt and freshly ground black pepper

Preheat your oven to 425°F and line a sheet pan with parchment paper for the croutons.

In a mixing bowl, combine the bread, 3 tablespoons of olive oil, garlic powder, and however much salt and pepper you and your cardiologist are comfortable with. Mix it by hand until the bread is evenly coated, then transfer to the prepped baking sheet, making sure not to overcrowd the pan because then they won't get crispy and fulfill their preordained destiny of becoming croutons. Bake until golden brown and crunchy, about 10 to 12 minutes, then remove from the oven and set aside.

To make the dressing, add the garlic, anchovy, Dijon mustard, Worcestershire sauce, lemon juice, and mayonnaise into a mixing bowl and give it a stir. Slowly pour the remaining olive oil into the mixture while whisking constantly until, through a combination of emulsification and black magic, it turns into a creamy, smooth dressing.

To assemble, add the romaine to a large salad bowl and pour in half the dressing. Toss the salad, then taste it. If it feels underdressed, add more dressing; if it feels overdressed, add more lettuce; if it tastes perfect, you're welcome. Add the cheese, croutons, and a shitload of fresh cracked pepper; give it a light toss; then taste again and adjust the seasoning as needed. If you'd like to add a flair of Roman authenticity, find and murder the son of God and then blame it on the Jews.

Serves 4

BLAT Salad

Most meal salads should be approached with extreme skepticism because salads are either appetizers that merely prepare your mouth for a more flavorful future or penance for eating too much and needing to lose weight. This is not one of those salads. This is a put-on-weight salad, a make-you-feel-lethargic-gassy-and-bloated (in a good way)-after-eating salad. It's basically a bacon lettuce avocado tomato sandwich that you clumsily spilled all over the counter, then hastily swept into a bowl and called a salad. There's even bread, but now that it's in a salad, we call it "croutons." It's bright, bacony, and filling, and even though it's packed with bacon, croutons, mayo, cheese, and avocado, it's a salad, so it must be good for you.

12 slices applewood
  smoked bacon
½ loaf crusty French bread,
  cut into 1-inch cubes
3 tablespoons mayonnaise
3 tablespoons sour cream
1 clove garlic, minced
2 tablespoons fresh lemon
  juice
4 tablespoons olive oil
1 tablespoon chopped fresh
  parsley

3 romaine hearts, chopped
1 pound cherry tomatoes,
  halved
½ cup kalamata olives,
  halved and pitted
1 large avocado, diced
½ cup Parmesan cheese
  shavings, divided
Kosher salt and freshly
  ground black pepper

Preheat your oven to 425°F and line a sheet pan with aluminum foil. Lay the bacon on the sheet pan and bake for 15 minutes, until it's crispy or stray dogs show up at your door. Transfer the bacon to a plate lined with paper towels, reserving the pan with bacon fat.

Scatter the bread on the reserved baking sheet, being careful not to burn yourself. Toss with tongs until the bread is evenly coated, then season with salt and pepper and bake until golden brown and crispy, about 10 minutes. Taste a crouton. If it's not crunchy, bake for another 2 minutes and repeat until it is. We do not tolerate non-crispified croutons.

In a mixing bowl, combine the mayonnaise, sour cream, garlic, and lemon juice and season with salt and pepper. Whisk vigorously and slowly pour in the olive oil. Continue whisking until the dressing is thick and fully combined. If your arms hurt while whisking, it's a good thing you're making a salad, fatty; maybe you should also hit the gym. Add the parsley, whisk to combine, and set the dressing aside.

In a large salad bowl, combine the romaine, tomatoes, kalamata olives, avocado, and half of the dressing. Toss the salad until the lettuce is evenly dressed, then taste and adjust the seasoning with salt and pepper as needed. To serve, divide the dressed salad among four plates. Crumble 3 slices of bacon over each—more if you like to party—then top with croutons, ¼ of the Parmesan cheese shavings, and a spoonful or two of the dressing. Serve immediately; every minute you waste makes the salad exponentially worse, so stop reading this and hurry up.

Serves 4

Chopped Salad

Kids are universally stupid. I was no exception.
When I was a kid, I earnestly believed that if you
ate something unhealthy, you could eat something
of approximately equal size that was healthy, and
the two things would cancel each other out. This
recipe is that idiotic childhood belief manifested
in salad form. It has healthy ingredients that will
stave off certain death for another day or so but
also taste like adulthood feels, counteracted by
delicious unhealthy ingredients that will make you
forget that you're eating a salad for a meal.

5 tablespoons extra-virgin olive oil

3 tablespoons apple cider vinegar

1 teaspoon honey

1 teaspoon Dijon mustard

1 garlic clove, minced

½ teaspoon crushed red pepper flakes

1 head radicchio, thinly sliced

1 head escarole, thinly sliced

½ cup kalamata olives, chopped

4 ounces provolone cheese, sliced into thin ribbons

4 ounces fennel salami (finocchiona), quartered, thinly sliced

Kosher salt and freshly ground black pepper

Start with the dressing. In a large salad bowl, combine the olive oil, apple cider vinegar, honey, Dijon mustard, garlic, and red pepper flakes. Whisk everything together until it's all combined and emulsified and looks like salad dressing. Season the dressing with salt and pepper, then taste it and adjust the seasoning as necessary.

Add the radicchio, escarole, olives, cheese, and salami to the salad bowl. Toss the ingredients until everything is equally coated with the dressing, making sure to reserve a few well-timed salad-tossing jokes for anyone lucky enough to pass through your kitchen.

Serves 4

Ginger, Chicken, and Rice Porridge

If chicken soup went to China, fell in love with congee, and, despite warnings from both of their families on the difficulties of intercultural souplationships, ran away together and had a baby, that baby would be this soup. It's like a warm consensual hug for your insides that will give you the soup-sweats and also the feeling that if a soup and a porridge can find love in this crazy world, then maybe you can too.

2 tablespoons vegetable oil	1 pound boneless skinless
1 white onion, finely chopped	chicken thighs
3 garlic cloves, minced	1 large bunch Swiss chard, stemmed, thinly sliced
1 (2-inch) piece ginger, minced	Juice of 1 lemon
1 teaspoon crushed red pepper flakes	1 bunch scallions, finely chopped
8 cups chicken broth	Sesame oil, for serving
¾ cup white rice, rinsed obsessively for 1 minute	Kosher salt and freshly ground black pepper

Put a stockpot over medium heat and add the vegetable oil. Add the onion and cook until it turns translucent and someone in your house comments, "It smells really good in there. What are you making?"— about 5 minutes. Add the garlic, ginger, and red pepper flakes and sauté for 2 more minutes, stirring occasionally so that the garlic doesn't burn. Add to the pot the chicken broth, the rice that you definitely rinsed until the water ran clear, the chicken, and a whole bunch of salt. Let everything boil, then turn the heat down to low and let it simmer uncovered for 20 minutes.

Using tongs or a supernaturally calloused hand, remove the chicken from the pot and let it cool until it doesn't burn you when you touch it. When it's cool enough to handle, use two forks or your bare hands to shred the meat into small pieces.

Add the Swiss chard and shredded chicken to the pot and simmer for 5 minutes. Add the lemon juice, taste it, and adjust the seasoning with salt and pepper as needed. To serve, divide the soup-congee lovechild among four bowls and top with a big spoonful of chopped scallions and a drizzle of sesame oil.

Serves 4

Cauliflower Soup

Cauliflower is gross. It looks like mutant mold, tastes like the inside of my mouth, and makes me gassy and bloated whenever I've had the misfortune of ingesting it, although that could just be my Judaism. Cauliflower is far and away the worst flower, but this soup is so damn good. It's rich and porky, requiring but one single pot, and it's easy enough that even you can make it. As is often the case with vegetables, when combined with bacon, cheese, and heavy cream, as well as a cook with a glint in their eyes and a soup in their heart, it can taste way, way less bad than on its own. So if you hate cauliflower, first of all good on ya, it's the worst, but second of all, try this soup—you'll change your mind, sorta.

½ pound applewood
  smoked bacon, chopped
1 large white onion, diced
2 shallots, chopped
1 medium carrot, chopped
4 garlic cloves, sliced

1 large head cauliflower,
  cut into 1-inch pieces
4 cups chicken broth
1 Parmesan cheese rind,
  washed
Kosher salt and freshly
  ground black pepper

Sauté the bacon in a stockpot or large saucepan over medium heat until it starts to brown and fills your house with a heavenly aroma that will make any vegetarian in your home switch teams. Add the onion, shallots, carrot, and garlic to the pot and cook until the vegetables soften and start to brown, about 8 to 10 minutes. Stir occasionally; don't let the bacon burn, or you will have that pig's blood on your hands.

Add the dreaded cauliflower, cursing it as it goes into the pot, along with the broth and cheese rind. Bring everything to a boil, then reduce the heat to medium-low, cover the pot, and simmer for 20 minutes.

Remove the soup from the heat. Using a slotted spoon, fish out the cheese rind and discard it or reserve it for someone you hate. Using a stick or regular blender or food processor, purée until smooth and creamy. Taste the soup, add salt and pepper until it tastes better than you thought you were capable of, then serve.

Serves 4

Corn Soup

I grew up in a soup-for-dinner family and therefore assumed that every other person in these great United States and other freedom-loving countries did too. This is one of my favorite dishes to make in the summer when the corn is sweet and fresh, but when I made it for friends who were visiting from out of town, they looked at me in horror. "But what's for dinner?" They were incredulous. "Soup is an appetizer. We flew all the way across the country to come see you and you make us . . . soup?" I reassured them that I was far more cultured than they were and that their ignorance was making them look bad, and then I made them this soup, which tastes like corn got really, really tasteful high-end cosmetic surgery. It's pure corn flavor, just enhanced a little bit to be the best version of itself. After one bowl, my ignorant friends became slightly less ignorant, and now they too are soup-for-dinner people.

1 stick unsalted butter	2 tablespoons extra-virgin
1 large white onion, thinly	olive oil
sliced	¼ teaspoon cayenne pepper
4 garlic cloves, minced	¼ teaspoon smoked paprika
10 ears corn, kernels	¼ teaspoon chili powder
removed and divided,	½ cup chopped fresh
cobs reserved	parsley
4 cups chicken stock	Kosher salt and freshly
½ cup heavy cream	ground black pepper
Juice of ½ lime	

Put a stockpot over medium heat and add the butter. When the butter starts to bubble, add the onion and garlic and sauté for 5 minutes. Add all but 1 cup of the corn kernels, the reserved cobs, and the chicken stock. Increase the heat to medium-high and bring everything to a boil, then reduce the heat to medium-low, cover the pot, and simmer for 30 minutes.

After 30 minutes, remove the cobs from the soup using tongs, being careful not to drop them into the liquid-magma soup, thereby burning yourself and any others within a Shamu-sized splash zone. Discard the cobs, stir in the heavy cream, and simmer for another 5 minutes.

Pull the soup off the heat and purée it until smooth using an immersion blender, regular blender, or food processor. Add the lime juice, then taste the soup and adjust the seasoning as necessary.

Put a heavy skillet over high heat. Add the olive oil, and when it begins to smoke, add the remaining 1 cup of corn kernels. Sauté for 3 minutes, stirring often, until lightly browned, then season with the cayenne, paprika, chili powder, salt, and pepper and cook for 1 more minute. To serve, ladle the soup into bowls and top with a heaping spoonful of the sautéed corn kernels and fresh parsley. Serve with bread or oyster crackers—or nothing else, because soup is a meal and anyone who thinks otherwise is a spoiled bourgeois pig who will one day be cannibalized by the working class.

Serves 4

Sausage, Escarole, and White Bean Soup

As a general rule of thumb, the worse something tastes, the healthier it is. Bitter greens, such as escarole, are packed with healthy science things that are proven to ensure you live a long, prosperous life in a tastefully renovated midcentury estate with seven groundskeepers and a devoted trophy spouse that you're allowed to trade in every ten years like a leased vehicle, provided you eat your daily allotment. But eating enough bitter greens to attain this ideal is difficult, mostly because they taste like shit. This soup is packed with those promising greens, whose general awfulness is masked by hot Italian sausage, so much so that you'll be like, "Wow, maybe I like escarole?"—but trust me, you don't. You like Italian sausage, which, like the late, great Alan Rickman, makes absolutely anything it's in immeasurably better.

3 tablespoons olive oil, divided	2 heads escarole, roughly chopped
1 pound Italian hot sausage links	1 (15.5-ounce) can cannellini beans, rinsed
4 garlic cloves, thinly sliced	4 cups chicken stock
½ teaspoon crushed red pepper flakes	Kosher salt and freshly ground black pepper

In a large heavy skillet, heat 1 tablespoon of olive oil over medium heat. When the oil begins to smoke, add the hot sausage links and cook, turning frequently, for 10 minutes. Remove the sausage from the pan, transfer to a plate lined with paper towels, and let them rest for 5 minutes.

Return the skillet to the heat and add 2 tablespoons of olive oil. Add the sliced garlic and sauté until it just starts to brown, about 1 minute. Don't burn the garlic, or I will come to your house and chastise you in a deeply personal, hurtful manner. I'm good at that; ask my wife. Add the red pepper flakes, escarole, cannellini beans, and chicken stock and let everything come to a boil.

While the soup is heating up, thinly slice the cooked sausage. Don't freak out if it's raw in the middle; it's going to be cooked in the soup for more than enough time to not kill you via food-borne illness. Add the sausage to the soup. When it comes to a boil, reduce the heat to medium-low and cover. Let it simmer for 20 to 30 minutes, then taste it and adjust the seasoning with salt and pepper until it's whatever version of salty you like to obscure the bitter shittiness of escarole.

Serves 4

Grilled Cheese and Tomato Soup

I can feel your judgment. You're thinking, "I didn't buy a cookbook so that this handsome, great-smelling, talented Jew could teach me how to make grilled cheese and tomato soup. Tomato soup comes in a can, and even I know how to make grilled cheese!" First of all, that's racist. Second of all, you'd make swill on your own unsupervised. And third, how dare you? In about 30 minutes, you'll have a big pot of homemade soup that's infinitely better than what comes in a can and a bunch of cheesy sandwiches to dip in it, so maybe instead of your judgment and dogshit attitude you buck up and show some appreciation before I pack it up and take my recipes elsewhere.

1 stick (4 ounces) unsalted	2 tablespoons granulated
butter, divided	sugar
1 medium red onion, diced	8 slices white bread
1/3 cup tomato paste	1 pound sliced American
2 (28-ounce) cans crushed	cheese
tomatoes	1/2 cup heavy cream
4 cups chicken broth	Kosher salt and freshly
1 bay leaf	ground black pepper

Put a stockpot over medium-high heat and add 4 tablespoons of butter. When the butter starts to bubble, add the red onion and cook, stirring often, for 5 minutes. Add the tomato paste, stirring so that it coats the onions, and cook for 2 more minutes. Add the tomatoes, broth, bay leaf, and sugar, and season with salt and pepper. Taste and adjust the seasoning until you like how it tastes. Bring to a boil, then reduce the heat to low and simmer for 20 minutes, stirring occasionally.

Start building your sandwiches by aggressively buttering one side of each slice of bread. This will be the outside of each sandwich, and even though I have taken great pains to notate that, I bet you five American dollars that you screw this up on *at least* one of your sandwiches. Top the unbuttered side with 1/4 of the American cheese, then sandwich it with another slice of bread, butter side out, and repeat. If you don't like American cheese, you're doing it wrong, and I'm not sure that we can be friends.

Heat a large, heavy skillet over medium heat and add the sandwiches. Cook them for 3 minutes, then flip them, cover the skillet, and cook for 3 more minutes, until the cheese is melted and the bread has a nice golden-brown crispy crunch. If your cheese isn't melting it's probably because you're substituting out the most meltable freedom-loving cheese with something else; in this case, add a few drops of water to the edge of the pan and cover it—the steam will help melt the cheese. Be careful not to let the water touch the bread, or you will have destroyed the crispity crunchiness that we have worked so hard to achieve.

Pull the soup off the heat and add the heavy cream. Purée until smooth with an immersion blender, regular blender, or food processor. Taste it and adjust the salt and pepper until you acquiesce to the fact that I was right. Cut the sandwiches into dunkable pieces and serve alongside the soup.

Makes 4 sandwiches and a bunch of soup

Reuben Sandwich

Jews love food that will ruin your day. Nowhere is this more evident than the Reuben sandwich. A proper Reuben requires you to clear your schedule for four to six hours after consumption because digestion is going to be an adventure. Your stomach will sound like a wounded wookiee; your body will go into survival mode as it devotes every last joule of energy to dealing with the ticking time bomb in your stomach; you will become gassy, bloated, and lethargic; and you will question every decision that led to you eating such a sandwich. And yet, somehow, it will all be worth it.

½ cup mayonnaise
5 tablespoons ketchup
2 tablespoons finely
  chopped dill pickles
1 tablespoon finely minced
  onion
1 tablespoon fresh lemon
  juice
1 tablespoon horseradish
1 teaspoon Worcestershire
  sauce

6 tablespoons unsalted
  butter, or as needed, at
  room temperature
8 slices marble rye bread
1 pound corned beef, thinly
  sliced
1 ½ cups sauerkraut,
  drained
8 slices Swiss cheese

Russia's greatest contributions to the world are the presidential pee tapes, the invention of the television, and Russian dressing. Combine the mayonnaise, ketchup, pickles, onion, lemon juice, horseradish, and Worcestershire sauce in a small bowl and mix until fully combined and able to influence a presidential election through a coordinated disinformation campaign. Set aside, but keep a very suspicious eye on it.

To make the sandwich, butter one side of each piece of bread with enough butter that you get chest pains just from spreading it. This will be the outside of the sandwich; don't screw this up and make it the inside, or the bread won't get crispy. Spread 2 tablespoons of Russian dressing on the unbuttered side, then top it with 4 ounces of corned beef, ¼ cup of sauerkraut, and 2 slices of cheese. Top all that with another piece of single-side-buttered bread, butter facing up. Repeat with the rest of the bread, beef, kraut, and dressing.

Put a heavy skillet over medium heat and add the assembled sandwiches. Cook until golden brown and crispy underneath, about 3 to 5 minutes. Flip the sandwiches and cook for 3 minutes more. The cheese should be melted, the bread should be golden, and your kitchen should smell and feel like a Jewish deli, but hopefully with a lot less complaining about prices.

Makes 4 sandwiches

Croque Madame

This recipe is really two recipes in one (you're welcome), because a croque madame can become a croque monsieur through either a series of costly hormone therapies and cosmetic surgeries that are not covered by insurance or by simply omitting the egg from this recipe. The secret to a croque madame is the béchamel sauce, which sounds hard to make because it's spelled with an accent mark, which we don't have in America, but just ignore that; it's super easy. Without the béchamel, this is just a lackluster ham and cheese sandwich that for some reason has a fried egg on top. But with the béchamel, it becomes a lovely stroll down the Champs-Élysées in springtime, past the chic boutiques, vibrant and bustling cafés, and a National Front white pride rally led by Marine Le Pen. You'll feel like you're really there.

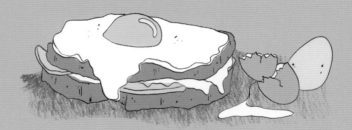

12 tablespoons unsalted
   butter, divided
2 tablespoons all-purpose
   flour
1⅓ cups whole milk
1 bay leaf
¼ teaspoon freshly grated
   nutmeg

¼ cup grated Parmesan
   cheese
8 slices country bread
8 slices ham
8 slices Gruyère cheese
4 eggs
Kosher salt and freshly
   ground black pepper

Preheat your oven to 300°F. Start with the béchamel sauce; that way if you screw up, you don't have to throw out the sandwiches, just the sauce. Put a saucepan over medium heat and melt 2 tablespoons of butter. When the butter starts to bubble, add the flour and whisk constantly for 2 minutes, then add the milk and bay leaf and whisk until any chunks are gone and the sauce is smooth. Bring the sauce to a boil, whisking constantly so it doesn't stick to the pan, then reduce the heat to low and cook for 2 more minutes. Remove from the heat and season to taste with salt, pepper, and freshly ground nutmeg. Discard the bay leaf, add the grated Parmesan cheese, and stir to combine.

To make the sandwiches, spread the béchamel sauce on the inside of 4 slices of bread. Don't skimp here, or it will be dry and disgusting, and it will be your fault because I warned you. Lay 2 slices of ham on each piece of béchameled bread, then top each with 2 slices of Gruyère and another piece of bread.

Put a heavy skillet over medium heat and melt a stick of butter in it. Brush the bread of the assembled sandwiches with the melted butter on both sides, then add the sandwiches to the pan. Don't crowd them. If you need to use two pans, use two pans. If you only have one pan, do this step in batches like an adult. Cook the sandwiches until the bread is golden brown, about 3 minutes, then flip them and cook for another 3 minutes. Add the skillet to the hot oven and cook until the cheese is melted and the béchamel bubbles, about 3 to 5 minutes.

Meanwhile, put a nonstick skillet over medium heat and add 2 tablespoons of butter. Add the eggs and fry for 2 to 3 minutes, until the white is set but the yolk is runny. Season with plenty of salt and pepper, top each sandwich with an egg, work a 35-hour week, then serve immediately.

Makes 4 sandwiches

Cavatelli with Creamy Leeks and Bacon

I live on the side of a mountain in the middle of nowhere. If you wanted to find me, you couldn't, and if you could, it's only because I let you. The only grocery store in town does 80 percent of their business in cigarettes and Busch tallboys, but they also stock a fairly narrow assortment of moldy vegetables and rancid meat for unsuspecting tourists. Fortunately, we have a farm stand nearby (shout-out to Migliorellis) that stocks their own fruits, vegetables, and meat they murder by hand themselves. The shelves get pretty bare in the winter save for some root vegetables, but somehow they always have leeks. This dish is basically a leek genocide. It's impossible to overbuy. It all just cooks down into a jammy, salty, cheesy sauce that is good all year round.

10 ounces cavatelli or whatever pasta you feel like; it won't matter

8 slices bacon, chopped into ½-inch pieces

2 pounds leeks, washed twice, quartered lengthwise, then sliced into ⅛-inch pieces

6 garlic cloves, thinly sliced

1 teaspoon crushed red pepper flakes

2 tablespoons unsalted butter

½ cup shredded Parmesan cheese

1 tablespoon fresh lemon juice

1 tablespoon fresh lemon zest

½ cup chopped fresh parsley

Kosher salt and freshly ground black pepper

Bring saltier-than-you-think-it-should-be water to a boil in a large saucepan and cook the pasta for however long the box tells you to.

Meanwhile, put a large heavy skillet over medium-high heat and add the chopped bacon. Cook until crispy, then remove with a slotted spoon and transfer to a plate covered in paper towels to drain, reserving the fat in the pan.

Lower the heat to medium; add the leeks, garlic, and red pepper flakes; and season with salt and pepper. Sauté, stirring occasionally, for about 15 minutes, until the leeks break down and become creamy and jammy. Taste it and adjust the salt until it fits your subjective definition of perfection.

Taste a piece of cavatelli or whatever pasta you're using; when it's to your liking, drain it, reserving 1 cup of the starchy pasta water.

Add the pasta to the skillet with the leeks, along with the butter and ¼ cup of the pasta water. Remove the skillet from the heat; add the cooked bacon, Parmesan cheese, lemon juice and zest, and parsley.

Stir until the pasta is coated in the sauce. If it's dry, add more of the pasta water ¼ cup at a time until it's reached your desired level of sauciness. If it's wet, return it to medium heat and cook until the extra liquid has cooked off. To serve, add a handful of chopped parsley to each bowl. Then take what you think is an unhealthy amount of Parmesan cheese, double it, and top everything with that.

Serves 4

Spaghetti alla 15 Minutes

This pasta is amazingly flavorful, unbelievably simple, and what I imagine my Italian grandmother would effortlessly whip up for a quick weeknight dinner if my Italian grandmother weren't actually a Jewish grandmother whose idea of cooking is scooping deli salads out of takeout containers from Publix, which is getting to be so expensive these days, you wouldn't believe it, I'm going to write a strongly worded letter to the manager!

12 ounces spaghetti
4 tablespoons olive oil
6 garlic cloves, minced
1 teaspoon red pepper
   flakes
4 oil-packed anchovy fillets
2 teaspoons capers, drained

2 tablespoons unsalted
   butter
Juice of ½ lemon
½ cup shredded Parmesan
   cheese
⅓ cup chopped fresh basil
Kosher salt and freshly
   ground black pepper

Put a pot of much-saltier-than-you-think-it-should-be water over high heat and bring to a boil. Add the spaghetti and cook it for however long the package recommends; I'm not a mind reader (well, I am a medium, which is like a mind reader, but you know what, that's a discussion for another day; let's stay on track here). Reserve 1 cup of the starchy water, and before you drain it, taste a piece of spaghetti and make sure it's done to your liking. Don't just blindly trust whatever Big Pasta tells you, sheeple.

In a large skillet over medium heat, add the olive oil, garlic, and red pepper flakes and sauté until the garlic just starts to brown, about 3 minutes. Add the anchovies and cook for 1 minute more. Add the capers, butter, and cooked spaghetti to the skillet along with ¼ cup of the pasta water. Stir until the pasta is fully coated in the sauce, then remove from the heat, squeeze half a lemon into the skillet, add the Parmesan cheese, and taste. Finish with a handful of fresh basil and adjust the seasoning with salt and pepper until it tastes like you are Italian or at the very least Jewish, which is basically just an Italian with worse food.

Serves 4

Dad's Mac and Cheese

John Golden only knows how to cook two dishes: mac and cheese and meatloaf.

According to him, any more than that would be effeminate or showy, and John Golden is neither of those things. His mac and cheese is the better of the two by a large margin. It's comforting, creamy, and crunchy, with enough cheese to put your cardiologist's kids through grad school.

I asked him his secret to making his mac and cheese, and he said—and mind you, this is a direct quote—"Make sure you don't fuck up the cheese sauce, or it will all be shit." So there you go. Good luck.

1 pound macaroni	2 ½ cups shredded smoked
3 tablespoons unsalted	Gruyère, divided
butter	½ teaspoon smoked paprika
3 tablespoons all-purpose	1 cup cornflakes or other
flour	unsweetened corn cereal
2 cups whole milk	Kosher salt and freshly
2 ½ cups shredded cheddar,	ground black pepper
divided	

Preheat your oven to 375°F and bring salty water to a boil in a large saucepan over high heat. Boil the macaroni for however long the package tells you. If you're like me and don't trust packages due to a traumatic childhood event, taste one and ensure doneness, then drain and set aside.

Now we make the sauce, which, remember, is important to not fuck up. In a saucepan over medium heat, melt the butter. When it starts to bubble, add the flour and stir constantly for 2 minutes. Pour in the milk and bring the mixture to a boil, then lower the heat to medium-low and let it simmer for 2 more minutes, stirring the entire time because you could really use the exercise. Add 2 cups of each shredded cheese and the smoked paprika and stir until the cheese has melted and the sauce is smooth and luxurious. Remove from the heat and taste it, then season with plenty of salt and pepper.

Pour the cooked macaroni into a Dutch oven or casserole dish and top it with half of the cheese sauce you just made perfectly because you followed my dad's directions. Stir until the pasta is coated in the sauce, then pour in the remaining cheese sauce. Sprinkle the remaining shredded cheese on top, then spread the cornflakes or whatever cereal you're using evenly over the entire dish.

Cover the Dutch oven or casserole dish with aluminum foil and bake for 25 minutes. The top should be slightly brown, the cheese sauce should be bubbling, and the sound of angelic singing should be heard throughout your kitchen. Remove from the oven and let cool for 5 minutes, unless you hate everyone you cooked for, in which case serve immediately and laugh at them as they scald their dumb mouths with the liquid-magma sauce.

Serves 6

Kimchi Fried Rice

Kimchi, ginger, soy sauce, and sriracha are like a cheat code to make anything they touch taste good. If you follow this recipe to a tee, it will turn out perfect; however, this is one of the rare occasions in this book where you can omit or substitute basically anything and still have it turn out satisfactory or better (I'm managing expectations, since you are the one cooking), provided you don't omit anything from the aforementioned cheat code. I make this recipe once a week, and I throw in whatever shit we have left over in the fridge—mushrooms, bacon, shrimp, cooked meats, tomatoes, leeks, broccoli, cabbage; you could put hot New York City summer garbage in here and it would somehow turn out delicious and probably also give you hepatitis C, but it would still be worth it.

2 cups white rice
4 tablespoons sesame oil,
  divided
5 eggs, beaten
2 medium carrots, peeled
  and cut into matchsticks
4 scallions, thinly sliced
1 (1-inch) piece ginger,
  peeled, finely minced

1 cup kimchi, roughly
  chopped
2 to 3 tablespoons soy
  sauce, or to taste
1 teaspoon fish sauce
1 lime, cut into wedges
Sriracha, for serving
Kosher salt and freshly
  ground black pepper

Start by cooking the rice. If you don't know how to do this, go to page 88 and learn how so that I don't have to repeat myself. While the rice is cooking, prep the rest of the ingredients.

Once the rice is finished cooking, put a nonstick skillet over medium heat. Add 1 tablespoon of the sesame oil and the beaten eggs and season with salt and pepper. Use a rubber spatula to keep the eggs moving in the pan and cook until the whites are set and they look like scrambled eggs (because they are), about 4 minutes. Transfer the eggs to a plate and reserve.

Put a large, heavy skillet or wok over medium-high heat. Add the remaining 3 tablespoons of sesame oil, and when it begins to smoke, add the carrots, scallions, and ginger. Sauté for 3 minutes, stirring occasionally, then add the kimchi, rice, soy sauce, and fish sauce. Mix everything up until combined and sauté for another 2 minutes. Taste it, and if it needs salt, add more soy sauce 1 teaspoon at a time until it tastes good. Then remove from the heat, add the eggs, and mix until incorporated. To serve, divide the fried rice among bowls and serve with thick wedges of lime and however much sriracha sauce your white-girl palate can handle.

Serves 4

Smoky Vegetable Personal Pizzas

If you were Italian you'd call this a *pizzetta*, which loosely translates to "little pizza that you won't screw up if you just follow Zach Golden's clear, concise instructions," but since you're probably not Italian we'll just call them personal pizzas. Personal pizzas, like pizza, are only as good as their dough, so considering your track record, definitely buy your dough fresh from a pizzeria. Don't get overconfident and try making it yourself from scratch, or you will ruin my nicely thought-out dish and probably leave me a one-star review for your troubles, and neither of us needs that kind of negativity in our lives right now.

2 medium potatoes, very
  thinly sliced
1 fennel bulb, very thinly
  sliced
½ red onion, very thinly
  sliced
6 ounces smoked Gouda
  cheese, grated
6 ounces smoked
  mozzarella cheese, grated

¼ cup all-purpose flour
Roughly 1 pound fresh
  pizza dough, definitely
  purchased from a pizzeria
4 tablespoons extra-virgin
  olive oil, divided
Kosher salt and freshly
  ground pepper

Preheat your oven to 435°F and line two sheet pans with parchment. Prep your vegetables and cheese. A twenty-dollar mandoline is ideal for getting very thin, consistently sized slices. A mandoline is also ideal for removing large amounts of flesh inadvertently, so use the handguard and keep your head on a swivel. Once the vegetables are prepped, salt the sliced potatoes lightly to draw out their water, which will help them get crispy.

Flour your work surface, divide your dough into 4 equal-sized pieces, and form them into balls. If your dough is too sticky to handle, add more flour to the work surface and your hands, 1 teaspoon at a time. Press each dough ball into a disc, then lightly stretch and rotate the dough until it forms a thin, 8- to 12-inch circle. Do not, under any circumstances, try to throw the pizza in the air, as this is an almost surefire way to ruin the dough, and knowing you, you probably forgot to buy a backup.

Put a heavy, ideally cast-iron, skillet over medium-high heat and add 1 tablespoon of olive oil. When the oil begins to smoke, add a dough round to the pan and cook for about 1 minute, until bubbles form on the top. Flip and cook for 1 more minute, then season with salt. Transfer to a sheet pan lined with parchment paper and repeat with the other 3 pizzas.

To assemble, layer the potato on the dough, overlapping the edges to cover the entire surface. Then, cover the potato with a layer of fennel, top the fennel with a layer of red onion, and then—because this is America—smother it all in cheese.

Season each pizza with salt and pepper and cook in the oven for 20 minutes. Let them cool for about 5 minutes, unless you want to burn the roof of your mouth, in which case slice and serve immediately.

Serves 4

Sweet and Sour Eggplant

The parts of the world that eat the grossest, most, shall we say, "exotic" meats usually have the best vegetarian dishes, and this Chinese-style eggplant is no exception. Eggplant is the perfect meat substitute—it's healthy-ish, tastes great, and has a toothsome bite that will remind you of that gleeful feeling of gnashing and tearing apart flesh with your bare teeth but without having to be complicit in the murder of an adorable little innocent animal.

2 cups white rice	1 (2-inch) piece ginger,
½ cup hoisin sauce	minced
4 tablespoons soy sauce	1 bunch scallions, tops and
2 tablespoons sesame oil	roots trimmed, chopped,
2 tablespoons rice vinegar	plus more for garnish
¼ cup canola oil	1 teaspoon red pepper
1 pound eggplant, cut into	flakes
1-inch chunks	Kosher salt and freshly
4 garlic cloves, minced	ground black pepper

Get a pot of white rice cooking. Go to page 88 if you cannot achieve the most basic of kitchen tasks, and please know that if it feels like you're being judged, it's because you are.

In a mixing bowl, combine the hoisin sauce, soy sauce, sesame oil, and rice vinegar and whisk to combine.

Put a large skillet over medium-high heat and add the canola oil. When it starts to smoke—not after it's been smoking for 3 minutes and your life expectancy plummets due to easily preventable smoke inhalation—add the eggplant to the skillet. Cook until the eggplant is golden brown and tender, stirring occasionally, about 6 minutes. Taste a piece of eggplant. If it's tough, cook it for another minute and repeat until the texture doesn't disgust you. If it's perfect, congratulations; you have earned my respect and may now move on to the next step.

Add the garlic, ginger, scallions, and red pepper flakes to the pan and sauté for 1 minute, stirring constantly so that it doesn't burn and ruin the dish. Add the sauce mixture and continue cooking until the sauce thickens and the eggplant is fully coated in it, about 2 minutes. Remove from the heat, taste, and adjust the seasoning as necessary with salt and pepper.

To serve, spoon the eggplant and sauce over a bowl of white rice, top with more chopped scallions, and loudly announce to any delicious animals within earshot that this dish saved their lives.

Serves 4

Vegetable Curry

I live deep in the heart of the Catskill Mountains in a secluded small town with a blindingly monochromatic population of 309. There are three restaurants, all owned by the same guy and all a slightly different version of Italian American food. So when I discovered that an Indian restaurant existed 35 miles away, it was one of the happier days of my life. For months, we'd do takeout at least once a week, driving an hour and a half to pick up spicy curries and neon-flavored meats, blasting the heat in the car to keep it warm on the long journey home. But then a friend of the owner, who for some reason was always in the restaurant, started messaging my wife on Instagram. Messages turned into pictures, and pictures turned into pictures of him in a Speedo, which, trust me, he was not pulling off, so we stopped going to the restaurant and started making curry at home. I'll be honest: I prefer the Indian restaurant's curry to mine, but what this dish lacks in authenticity it more than makes up for in preventing you from getting chopped into a bunch of pieces by some old white serial killer who preys on Indian food enthusiasts, so all in all, it's worth it.

2 cups white rice
1 tablespoon canola oil
1 cup diced potato
½ cup halved and thinly
  sliced carrots
½ cup red bell pepper, thinly
  sliced
1 (3-inch) piece ginger, finely
  grated
4 garlic cloves, minced
3 tablespoons Thai red curry
  paste

1 (14-ounce) can coconut
  milk
½ cup water
½ pound baby bok choy,
  quartered lengthwise
1 teaspoon fish sauce
1 lime
½ cup fresh cilantro
Kosher salt and freshly
  ground black pepper

Prepare a pot of white rice or, if you're a yuppie who just wants to watch the world burn, brown rice. If you don't know how to do this, go to page 88. We'll wait.

Put a large skillet over medium heat and add the canola oil. When the oil is hot, add the potato, carrot, bell pepper, ginger, garlic, and red curry paste and cook for 5 minutes, stirring occasionally. Add the coconut milk and water and let simmer for 5 minutes, then add the baby bok choy and fish sauce and cook for 3 to 5 minutes more, until the potato and carrots are tender. Taste one of each vegetable to check for doneness. Do not leave this to chance, or you risk undercooking the vegetables, and then, like, what are you even doing?

Remove the curry from the heat. Cut a lime in half; squeeze the juice from one half into the curry and slice the other half into 4 wedges for serving. Taste the curry and adjust the seasoning as needed with salt and pepper until it tastes like restaurant food. Divide among however many portions you feel like (no judgment if this is all for you, tubs), and serve with fresh cilantro, a wedge of lime, and almost no risk of being murdered.

Serves 4

Roasted Vegetable and Bacon Hash

If you're able to roughly chop vegetables (or alternatively, claw them apart with your bare hands) and turn on an oven, then congratulations—you have all the requisite skills to not fuck up this dish and will be treated to a healthy-ish, easy meal that absolutely nobody will believe you're capable of. And for the love of God, go online and buy as much Dinosaur BBQ Cajun Foreplay spice rub as you can afford; mortgage your children's future on it if you must. I promise you it will be worth it for this dish and all others.

3 to 4 medium potatoes,
  diced
2 large sweet potatoes,
  diced
3 to 4 medium beets, diced
¼ cup extra-virgin olive oil
Kosher salt and freshly
  ground pepper

3 tablespoons Dinosaur
  BBQ Cajun Foreplay
  spice rub, or lesser Cajun
  seasoning replacement
8 ounces bacon strips
¼ cup chopped fresh
  parsley

Preheat your oven to 425°F. Make sure you cut the potatoes, sweet potatoes, and beets into equal-sized ½-inch pieces so that they cook in the same amount of time. Place the diced vegetables on a sheet pan lined with parchment paper. Ask for consent and, if granted, give the vegetables a heavy golden shower of olive oil. Make sure not to overcrowd the sheet pan, or the vegetables won't get crispy, which would be a real shame that rests squarely on your shoulders. Use two sheet pans if you have to, but do not compromise on crispiness.

Season the vegetables with salt and pepper as well as a heavenly cascade of Dinosaur BBQ Cajun Foreplay spice rub, or whatever lesser Cajun or barbecue spice rub you decide to use because you didn't prepare ahead of time, even though it's available online with one-day shipping.

Roast the vegetables for 45 minutes, total. While they're cooking, line a sheet tray with aluminum foil and lay out the strips of bacon. Cook the bacon in the oven with the vegetables for the last 15 minutes of cooking. Remove both sheet trays from the oven. Let the vegetables cool. Transfer the bacon to a plate lined with paper towels, and be careful not to delay your meal with a visit to your local burn ward necessitated by an untimely grease burn.

Chop the bacon into ½-inch pieces and add them to the roasted vegetables. Mix it all together and serve, topping with however much fresh parsley you feel like.

Serves 4

Slow-Cooked Halibut with Chimichurri

This recipe requires you to say, "Low and slow, baby," ideally while imitating a morbidly obese southern barbecue pit master, no fewer than seven times during its preparation, and if you're not willing to do that, then keep moving—the dish just doesn't work without it. Low and slow cooking results in halibut that's extremely juicy, tender, and flavorful, but it also takes a long-ass time compared to hot and fast cooking. If you're extremely impatient, currently hangry, or know that for whatever reason you're destined to ruin some halibut and just want to get it over with quickly so that you still have time to order takeout, then this recipe probably isn't for you.

2 tablespoons grated lemon zest, divided
½ cup plus 2 tablespoons extra-virgin olive oil, divided
4 (4- to 6-ounce) halibut fillets
½ cup chopped fresh parsley
½ cup chopped fresh cilantro
3 garlic cloves, minced
1 teaspoon red pepper flakes
2 tablespoons red wine vinegar
Kosher salt and freshly ground black pepper

Preheat your oven to 250°F. Low and slow, baby! In a baking dish, combine half the lemon zest and 2 tablespoons of olive oil. Add the halibut fillets and coat them in the marinade, then season with more salt and pepper than you think necessary. Roast it in the oven for about 40 to 45 minutes (low and slow, baby!); then, using a fork, poke the thickest part of the fillet and gently twist. If it flakes, it's ready; if it's gooey or translucent, cook for 5 more minutes and recheck. If it's dry and overdone, sneak into a reclusive crackpot scientist's lab, befriend him by showing an interest in his experiments, and finally ride his modified DeLorean approximately 40 minutes into the past to right your wrong and unruin this beautiful dish.

While the halibut is in the oven, make the chimichurri. In a mixing bowl, combine the parsley, cilantro, garlic, red pepper flakes, red wine vinegar, the rest of the lemon zest, remaining olive oil, and a heavy dose of salt and pepper. Stir until everything is combined, then taste and adjust the seasoning. When the halibut is finished cooking, top it with the chimichurri and serve immediately because this took fucking forever and we're all hungry.

Serves 4

Ginger Scallion Salmon with Oyster Sauce

If you find cooking foreign cuisines intimidating, then shame on you for being so ethnocentric. Every culture has a magic sauce that you can put on anything to make it delicious. In the USA we have ketchup; in Korea there's gochujang; and in China, Thailand, and throughout much of Southeast Asia, it's oyster sauce, which, trust me, is a lot better tasting than it sounds. It's deep, earthy, salty, and sweet and can cover up even the most flagrant kitchen fuckups, making it the key to this dish.

2 cups white rice
2 tablespoons vegetable or
   canola oil
2 garlic cloves, thinly sliced
3 tablespoons fresh ginger,
   minced
2 bunches scallions, tops
   and roots trimmed, sliced
   into 1-inch-long pieces
1 teaspoon red pepper
   flakes
6 tablespoons oyster sauce

2 tablespoons soy sauce
4 (4- to 6-ounce) salmon
   fillets
1 tablespoon unsalted
   butter
1 lime, halved—half juiced,
   half cut into 4 wedges
1 tablespoon sesame seeds
1/3 cup fresh cilantro
Kosher salt and freshly
   ground black pepper

Get a pot of white rice cooking. If you can't do that by yourself, turn to page 88, and I'll hold your hand through it.

Put a large cast-iron or nonstick skillet over medium heat. Add the oil and when it just begins to smoke, add the garlic and ginger, stirring constantly for 1 minute. Add the scallions and red pepper flakes, season lightly with salt and pepper, and cook for 5 minutes more, stirring occasionally.

Add the oyster sauce and soy sauce and bring to a simmer. Season the fish lightly with salt and pepper. There is a fuckload of salt in the oyster sauce and soy sauce, so don't go overboard. Add the salmon to the pan and simmer for 5 minutes, then turn each piece once and only once and simmer for 5 more minutes. If the liquid starts to boil, reduce the heat to medium-low so that it doesn't burn and ruin the sauce. If the sauce gets thick and gloppy, add water a tablespoon at a time and stir until the sauce magically unruins itself.

Add the butter and the juice from half a lime into the skillet and swirl the pan until everything is nice and saucy. Cook for 2 more minutes, spooning the sauce over the fish to coat it in unfuckupable flavor.

To serve, arrange scallions atop white rice and top with a salmon fillet. Sprinkle the sesame seeds evenly over each salmon fillet, then spoon some sauce over the fish, finish with a wedge of lime and a handful of fresh cilantro, and reflect on why you didn't open your heart to oyster sauce sooner.

Serves 4

Shrimp Scampi

Nobody fucks up language quite like Italian Americans. The Italian American dialect sounds like your mouth got blackout drunk while your brain stayed sober. In Italian American, "fagioli" becomes *vasul*. "Ricotta" becomes *rigot*. "Capicola" becomes *gabbagool*. All the sounds are there, just garbled incoherently like a belligerent drunk trying to give directions to a cab driver while also eating a party-sized submarine sandwich meant for four people. Shrimp scampi is yet another delicious example of language mutilation. "Scampi" is another name for the Norway lobster, a species of lobster that's pale and blond and has naturally hairless genital areas, so "shrimp scampi" is like calling a dish "pork beef," or as it's pronounced by native Italian American speakers, *poraboolo*.

3 tablespoons olive oil	1½ pounds large shrimp,
3 tablespoons unsalted	peeled and deveined
butter	Juice of 1 lemon
8 garlic cloves, minced	½ cup chopped fresh
2 shallots, finely diced	parsley
½ cup dry white wine	4 slices crusty bread
½ teaspoon red pepper	Kosher salt and freshly
flakes	ground black pepper

Put a large heavy skillet over medium heat and add the olive oil and butter. When the butter is completely melted, add the garlic and shallots and sauté for 1 minute; don't let the garlic burn, or an Italian American person will show up at your door and gesticulate threateningly while assuring you that this is the Jets' year (it's not, but just let them tire themselves out). Add the wine and red pepper flakes and season with salt and a shitload of pepper. Cook for 2 minutes or until the liquid in the skillet has reduced by half.

Make sure your shrimp are dry, peeled, and deveined, which is a less disgusting way of saying cut its poop chute out of its body and remove it so that you're not eating shrimp doody, which isn't fancy. Add the shrimp to the skillet and sauté for 2 minutes, then flip and cook for 2 more minutes, until they turn pink and the flesh changes from translucent to opaque. Remember, if you overcook the shrimp, you can't undo that without significant advances in science, so err on the side of undercooking. Taste a shrimp to check doneness; you can always cook it a little longer.

When the shrimp are perfectly cooked, remove them from the heat, add the fresh lemon juice and parsley, and stir until everything is combined. Taste a shrimp and adjust the seasoning with salt and pepper as needed. Serve with some crusty bread to sop up the juices or some pasta if you're too good for bread.

Serves 4

Mussels with Andouille, Fennel, and Grape Tomatoes

Mussels look fucking gross. They're sea insects with furry hipster beards and look like diseased skin tags ripped straight out of my nightmares. But in spite of looking gross, mussels are also delicious when paired with less gross ingredients; are able to be raised sustainably, which is important as we enter the apocalyptic phase of human existence; and are exceedingly difficult to fuck up, so put on a blindfold or just suck it up because it's what's for dinner. This recipe uses andouille sausage to add a bold, meaty, spicy kick to the broth and distract you from the harsh visual reality of your main ingredient. Think of it as the perfect mussels dish for people who hate mussels.

2 tablespoons olive oil
12 ounces spicy andouille
  sausage, thinly sliced
½ white onion, thinly sliced
1 fennel bulb, thinly sliced
4 garlic cloves, crushed
8 ounces cherry tomatoes,
  halved
1 cup dry white wine
4 pounds mussels,
  debearded and scrubbed
(toss any that are open
  and don't close when
  squeezed)
2 tablespoons unsalted
  butter
2 tablespoons chopped
  fresh parsley
Bread for serving
Kosher salt and freshly
  ground black pepper

Put a lidded saucepan or stockpot large enough to hold all the mussels over medium heat. Add the olive oil and when it just begins to smoke add the andouille. Cook the andouille until it starts to brown and get crispy, stirring frequently, about 5 minutes. Add the onion and fennel and cook for 5 minutes more, then add the garlic and cook for 1 minute. Be careful not to burn the garlic, or the dish will be ruined, and even though you'll be relieved that your meal won't feel like the second challenge on *Fear Factor*, it will be a damn shame.

Add the cherry tomatoes and white wine and bring everything to a simmer. Cook until the liquid is reduced by about half, about 5 minutes. Add the mussels, being sure not to make eye contact. Cover the pot and cook until the mussels pop open, another 5 to 8 minutes. Throw away any mussels that don't open, or you will die instantly from paralytic shellfish poisoning, or maybe you won't, but do you really want to risk it? Taste the broth and adjust the seasoning with salt and freshly ground pepper. If it gets too dry, add a splash more wine and let it cook down for 1 minute. Remove from the heat, add the butter, and stir until the sauce gets smooth and creamy.

Divide the mussels and broth among four bowls and top each with chopped fresh parsley. Serve with crusty, thickly sliced bread to sop up the liquid, then turn all the lights off and tell whoever you're eating with that with the deprivation of one sense (in this case, vision), the others are heightened, or whatever suitable lie you come up with to distract from the mussels.

Serves 4

Buffalo Wings Made Correctly

Buffalo wings are my favorite food, but not when you make them. They are one of the easiest things on the planet to make, and yet 99.9 percent of the world's population are incapable of not fucking them up. Usually, the beauty of cooking is that you get to improvise, break rules, and put your twist on recipes, but this is emphatically not the case with buffalo wings. Some rules: First, if you bread your wings, I will come to your house and start a grease fire. Second, blue cheese is the only acceptable dipping sauce for buffalo wings; you cannot have ranch. Third, don't bake, grill, or air fry your wings; you deep-fry them, and you live with the consequences. Fourth, prior to eating your wings, you must first say a blessing to the patron saint of quarterbacking, Joshua Allen, and the magnificent Buffalo Bills.

2 to 4 cups canola oil, depending on the size of your pot

2/3 cup Frank's Original Red Hot Sauce

1 stick unsalted butter

1 ½ tablespoons white vinegar

¼ teaspoon Worcestershire sauce

½ teaspoon Tabasco sauce

¼ teaspoon cayenne pepper

1/8 teaspoon garlic powder

3 pounds chicken wings, split into flats and drumsticks

Blue cheese dressing, for serving

3 spears celery, halved lengthwise and cut into 4-inch sticks

1 carrot, peeled, quartered lengthwise, and cut into 4-inch sticks

Kosher salt and freshly ground black pepper

Put a large stockpot over medium-high heat and add enough oil to fill it by at least 3 inches. Heat the oil to 375°F, using a cooking thermometer to make sure you're up to temp. If the oil is too cold, the wings won't get crispy and will be limp and gross. If the oil is too hot, the wings will burn or be raw in the middle, which is also gross. And, oh yeah, be careful: a big pot full of hot oil is the cooking equivalent of juggling three loaded pistols with the safety off, so pay attention.

While the oil is heating up, put a heavy skillet over medium heat. Add the Frank's Red Hot, butter, white vinegar, Worcestershire sauce, Tabasco sauce, cayenne pepper, garlic powder, salt, and pepper. Whisk everything together until the butter is melted and everything is combined, then taste it and adjust the seasoning to your tastes. If you want it to be hotter, add more cayenne. If you want it milder, omit the cayenne pepper entirely and then question all the life decisions that brought you to this point.

Fry the wings in batches in the oil for 8 minutes, not crowding the pot. If you followed instructions, that will be the perfect amount of time. Using a slotted spoon, transfer them to a plate lined with paper towels.

In a large mixing bowl, combine the wings and sauce, tossing until they are evenly coated in a heavenly layer of orange bliss. Serve immediately with blue cheese, celery, and carrots, and reflect on how the Bills make you want to shout, kick your heels up and shout, throw your hands up and shout, throw your head back and shout, c'mon now, the Bills are making it happen now.

Serves 4 to 6

Vietnamese-Style Grilled Pork Kabobs with Vermicelli

Vietnam has the best food on the planet: fight me. I should mention that I've never actually been to Vietnam because humidity doesn't do great things for my hair, but I have ordered an unhealthy amount of Vietnamese takeout from restaurants where the menu is just pictures of dishes with numbers (which is a telltale sign that a restaurant will be good), and I have an above-average imagination, so I feel like I've been there and thus am entitled to teach you how to cook their food authentically.

3 garlic cloves, minced
1 shallot, chopped
1 (2.5-inch) piece fresh
  ginger, peeled
1 tablespoon light brown
  sugar
1 tablespoon fish sauce
¼ cup soy sauce
4 tablespoons olive oil

1 large pork tenderloin,
  cut into ½-inch pieces
  then halved
1 package vermicelli
  noodles
Lime wedges, for serving
Chopped fresh mint, for
  serving
Kosher salt and freshly
  ground black pepper

Add the garlic, shallot, ginger, brown sugar, fish sauce, soy sauce, olive oil, and a pinch of salt and pepper into a blender, food processor, or if you live in a *Flintstones* cartoon, a piranha's mouth. Blend it for 10 to 15 seconds, then pour the marinade into a large plastic bag. Add the pork to the bag and coat the pieces in the marinade, then seal the bag and let everything mingle for at least 30 minutes and up to 12 hours.

Light your grill, clean the grates, and lightly oil the cooking surface. If you don't have a grill, either get one or substitute a grill pan or heavy skillet. Set your grill to medium-high and let it come to temperature. If you're fancy and your grill has a thermometer, aim for 400° to 450°F.

If you're using wooden skewers, soak them in cold water for 30 minutes so they don't burn on the grill. Thread the pieces of pork onto the skewers, 4 or 5 pieces per skewer. Cook for 7 minutes, then flip and cook 7 more minutes. You're looking for a crispy light char without overcooking. If you're unsure and weak-willed, you can cut into the meat and peek, but with that knowledge you sacrifice juiciness, and trust me, friend-o: it ain't worth it. Remove from the grill and let rest.

Cook the vermicelli noodles in boiling water according to the package instructions. Serve the meat on the skewer over the noodles. Top with fresh chopped mint and a wedge of lime, and now that you're an expert in Vietnamese cuisine, lecture anyone who will listen about the proper pronunciation of "pho."

Serves 4

Chicken Milanese with Baby Arugula Salad

This dish is basically bourgie chicken fingers, but that doesn't sound nearly as impressive as chicken Milanese, so let's just keep that as our little secret. You'll be working with raw chicken here, and raw chicken is the puffer fish of the land. When handled correctly, it's delicious; but when handled incorrectly, your dish will come with a surprise side of bloody stools, painful cramping, and, in extreme cases, the sweet release of death, so wash your hands and cook your chicken to 165°F.

4 boneless skinless chicken
  breasts
½ cup all-purpose flour
3 large eggs, beaten
2 cups panko breadcrumbs
¼ cup grated Parmesan
  cheese
¼ cup plus 2 tablespoons
  extra-virgin olive oil,
  divided

1 tablespoon fresh lemon
  juice
2 teaspoons Dijon mustard
4 cups baby arugula
1 lemon, cut into wedges for
  serving
Kosher salt and freshly
  ground black pepper

Pound out the chicken by laying each breast between two pieces of plastic wrap and smashing the ever-living hell out of it with a meat pounder or something heavy and solid until the breast is about ¼ inch thick. Season each of the pounded breasts with lots of salt and pepper.

Prep your breading station: pour the flour on a plate, beat the eggs in a large bowl, and combine the panko and grated Parmesan cheese in a shallow dish.

Dip each pounded breast in the flour and shake off the excess. Dunk them in the beaten egg until fully coated and let the excess run off, then place in the panko mixture and coat both sides with crispity-bits until, much like Mormon pornography, the breasts are fully covered.

In a large skillet heat ¼ cup of the olive oil over medium-high heat. When the oil starts to smoke, add the chicken, 2 breasts at a time, making sure not to overcrowd the pan. Fry until the bottoms are golden brown, about 3 minutes, then flip and cook for another 3 minutes. Transfer to a plate lined with paper towel and season immediately with a shitload of salt.

In a mixing bowl, combine the remaining 2 tablespoons of olive oil, fresh lemon juice, and Dijon mustard. Whisk vigorously until it looks like salad dressing, then season lightly with salt and pepper. Add the arugula to the mixing bowl and toss until coated, then top each chicken breast with a big handful of the dressed arugula salad and a lemon wedge, and deny, deny, deny if someone accuses you of making chicken fingers.

Serves 4

Utica Greens

Utica is a small rust-belt city nestled in the Mohawk Valley of New York. It's a working-class area with eight months of winter, and its primary industries are farming and cooking (meth). My dad grew up outside of Utica, and whenever some unknown relative whose name sounded like a minor character in Fiddler on the Roof died, we'd visit to pay our respects and also sample some of the region's finest delicacies. For the shithole that it is, Utica has a surprising number of excellent signature foods: tomato pies, half-moon cookies, and the eponymous Utica greens. This recipe takes a giant pile of escarole and adds salty, pickley, crunchy, meaty, cheesy distractions that turn a lackluster bitter green into something so good that you'll seriously consider visiting Utica, New York, before realizing how ridiculous that sounds and abandoning the idea.

2 heads escarole, roughly
    chopped
½ cup plus 2 tablespoons
    extra-virgin olive oil,
    divided
1 cup breadcrumbs
1 cup grated Parmigiano-
    Reggiano, divided

½ cup prosciutto, finely
    chopped
8 pickled cherry peppers,
    roughly chopped
4 garlic cloves, minced
Kosher salt and freshly
    ground black pepper

Preheat your broiler to high and place a rack at the top of the oven. Bring a large pot of salted water to boil over high heat. Taste it while salting; if it doesn't make you dry heave, it's not salty enough. When it's at a rolling boil, add the escarole and cook for 1 minute, then pour it into a colander, rinse with cold water, and set aside to let drain.

In a mixing bowl combine ½ cup of the olive oil, the breadcrumbs, and ½ cup of the Parmigiano-Reggiano cheese. Mix it together until it has the texture of wet sand; if you're unsure, spoon some between your butt cheeks and roll around. If it chafes, it's perfect; if it doesn't chafe, add more breadcrumbs to the mixture until it does.

Put a large heavy skillet over medium heat and add the remaining 2 tablespoons of olive oil. When the oil starts to smoke, add the prosciutto, cherry peppers, and garlic and sauté for 5 minutes. If the garlic cooks too quickly and starts to burn, reassure it and yourself that everything will be okay through positive visualization, or just lower the heat a bit. Add the blanched greens to the skillet and season with salt and pepper. Cook for 5 minutes, then taste it and adjust the seasoning as necessary.

Sprinkle the breadcrumbs evenly on top but don't stir it in; you want it to get crunchy under the broiler. Transfer the skillet to the top rack of the oven just under the broiler and cook for 2 to 3 minutes, until the top has browned. Remove from the broiler and top with the remaining Parmigiano-Reggiano cheese, and be glad a distant relative didn't have to die for you to get this delicious meal.

Serves 2

Briny Sheet Pan Chicken

Love is all about compromise. My wife hates olives, but I love them. So to compromise, I secretly cook with them and just remove them from the dish right before serving so that there's no visual proof, and then she's all like, "Mmmm, this is so good . . . I can't put my finger on what it tastes like, but whatever it is, it's amazing." If I try to tell her that what she can't put her finger on is, in fact, olives and the incredible briny, salty depth of flavor that they add to everything they come in contact with, she will instantly about-face and insist that she doesn't like the dish anymore because apparently I married a child who doesn't have the emotional maturity to appreciate how good olives are, so why the hell should I be the one who compromises?

2 pounds potatoes, sliced ⅛ inch thick	2 tablespoons capers, drained
4 tablespoons extra-virgin olive oil	4 ounces kalamata olives, pits removed, halved
2 teaspoon herbes de Provence	1 lemon, half juiced, half cut into wedges
8 bone-in, skin-on chicken thighs	Kosher salt and freshly ground black pepper

Preheat your oven to 450°F and prep a sheet pan by lining it with parchment paper. In a large mixing bowl, combine the potatoes that you definitely made sure to slice evenly so that they cook in the same amount of time, the olive oil, herbes de Provence, and a bunch of salt and pepper. Toss to combine, then arrange the potatoes in a single layer on the sheet pan. You can overlap the edges if you need to for space, but don't crowd them, you monster.

Season the chicken thighs with a shitload of salt and pepper on all sides, then rub your chicken-y hands all over any casual enemies while chanting, "Salmonella! Salmonella!" and doing a little kooky dance. Arrange the chicken thighs atop the potatoes, then distribute the capers and kalamata olives around evenly. Squeeze the juice from half a lemon atop everything and put it in the oven.

Roast until the chicken is crispy and cooked through and the potatoes are tender and golden brown, about 30 to 35 minutes. Remove from the oven and let rest for 5 minutes, then serve immediately with wedges of fresh lemon, making sure to discard olives prior to serving if you are married to a petulant, fussy child.

Serves 4

Korean-Style Flat Iron Steak with Pickled Shallots

Gochujang is Korean for "magic sauce," I think—I didn't actually check, but if it's not it definitely should be. It's spicy, sweet, salty, and kinda funky in a good way. The red chili sauce is a Korean staple that gives whatever it touches a sweet flavorful heat, making it the perfect condiment for shitty cooks such as yourself, because it does all the heavy lifting for you. For this recipe, if you can successfully navigate already killed meat and a few other ingredients into a bag, pickle onions, and light a grill without being investigated for arson, then you'll have an incredibly flavorful meal that makes you look worldly and capable, at least until you attempt to pronounce "gochujang."

태양초찰고추장

KOREAN GOCHUJANG
(RED PEPPER PASTE)

4 tablespoons gochujang paste, plus more for serving	1 flat iron steak, about 1½ pounds
4 tablespoons olive oil	4 large shallots, thinly sliced
4 tablespoons unseasoned rice vinegar	⅔ cup red wine vinegar
1 bunch scallions, tops and roots trimmed, thinly sliced, divided	Kosher salt and freshly ground black pepper

Start by making the marinade. In a large resealable plastic bag, combine the gochujang paste, olive oil, and rice vinegar. Add ½ of the scallions as well as a few aggressive pinches of salt and plenty of fresh pepper. Add the steak to the bag and give it a sensuous massage so that the marinade coats the meat and the ingredients get to know each other. Chill the steak for at least 30 minutes and up to 24 hours.

While the steak is chilling, combine the thinly sliced shallots with the red wine vinegar and a pinch of salt in a small mixing bowl. Congratulations, you have made pickled shallots. Let them sit for at least 30 minutes while you celebrate your accomplishment.

Prepare your grill by cleaning the grates and lightly oiling the cooking surface with an oil-soaked paper towel. Then light the grill. If you don't have a grill, either get one or substitute a grill pan or heavy skillet. Set your grill to medium-high and let it come to temperature, around 400°F to 450°F.

Remove the steak from the bag, letting any excess marinade drip off. For medium rare, grill it for 3 minutes, then flip it once and only once and grill for 3 minutes more, then remove it from the heat and let it rest for 10 minutes. You can vary the cooking times based on your desired level of doneness, but just know that you're blowing it if you cook it past medium and that my dad will think less of you.

Slice the steak against the grain and serve with pickled shallots and more gochujang. If you don't understand cutting against the grain, slice a small piece off the steak, look at which way the muscle fibers run, and cut perpendicular to them. If you still don't understand, just wing it; you have a 50 percent chance of being right and those odds aren't terrible.

Serves 4

Fennel, Sausage, Potato, and Scallion Sheet Pan Dinner

My wife is unbelievably beautiful, smart, and wonderful beyond compare. That said, she kinda fucking sucks at cooking. For the first five years we were together, she cooked for us a total of four times, and three of those times were the same dish (pastelón, look it up). But then she discovered sheet pan dinners, which are basically one-pot meals but the pot is a sheet pan. Now she cooks once a week, which she complains about at least twice a week, and this is her go-to dish. Trust me—if she can do it, you should have no trouble.

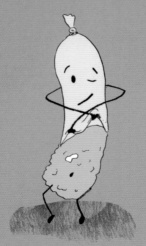

3 large potatoes, sliced into
⅛-inch slices
1 large red onion, sliced
into ½-inch pieces
1 bunch scallions, tops and
roots removed, chopped
2 fennel bulbs, sliced into
½-inch pieces

3 tablespoons extra-virgin
olive oil
12 ounces hot Italian
sausage, casings removed
½ lemon, juiced
Freshly grated Parmesan
cheese
Kosher salt and freshly
ground pepper

Preheat your oven to 425°F and line a sheet pan with parchment paper. Don't forget either of these steps, or this recipe will take twice as long, and you'll blame me even though that's a classic you-move.

Place the sliced potatoes on the sheet pan in a single layer, overlapping the edges if you need to for space. If you overcrowd the pan, you will ruin the dish before it even goes in the oven and will rightfully feel like an abject failure, so give them some space or use two sheet pans. Layer the onions, scallions, and fennel on atop the potatoes, then evenly coat everything with olive oil and season with a shitload of salt and pepper.

Remove the sausage from its casing and pinch it into small, roughly ½-inch pieces. Scatter the sausage nubbins around the sheet pan, then roast it all for 30 minutes. Let it rest for 5 minutes, then give it a squeeze of fresh lemon juice and top with however much freshly grated Parmesan cheese you feel like, being careful not to grate your finger, as blood and skin makes for a far less fancy topping than hard, salty cheese.

Serves 4

Green Curry Braised Chicken

Of all the dishes in this book, this one has the highest effort to perceived effort ratio (E:PE). That means that with very, very little effort, the resulting dish will taste like you spent all day cooking because that's just the kind of person you are, or at least how you want people to think of you, even though it's completely divorced from reality. All you have to do is chop a couple of things up, dump everything into a vessel that won't shatter and cause a not-so-delicious oven fire, and then sit back and let coconut milk, curry paste, and a couple of very special guest stars work their magic and make you look like you're capable of thinking about others for once, Karen.

2 (13.5-ounce) cans
    unsweetened coconut
    milk
6 tablespoons Thai green
    curry paste
Grated zest of 1 lemon
1 (3-inch) piece ginger,
    peeled, minced
6 garlic cloves, peeled
1 small jalapeño pepper,
    stalk removed

1 teaspoon fish sauce
8 boneless, skinless chicken
    thighs
1 pot of perfectly cooked
    rice
¼ cup chopped fresh
    cilantro
1 lime, cut into wedges
Kosher salt and freshly
    ground black pepper

Preheat your oven to 400°F. In a blender or food processor, combine the coconut milk, green curry paste, lemon zest, ginger, garlic, jalapeño, and fish sauce. Blend for 10 to 15 seconds until just combined.

Season all sides of the chicken with salt and pepper, but don't go too crazy; the curry paste is basically salt paste, and you can always add more later, while taking salt out after the fact requires finding a wrinkle in time, which can be quite time-consuming and distract from the dish. Add the chicken to a baking dish or high-walled skillet and pour the sauce over it. Bake for 1 hour, spooning liquid over the chicken every 15 minutes. You should probably set a timer; I don't trust you to remember on your own.

Serve the chicken over white rice that you definitely did not fuck up because you went to page 88 and followed the recipe. Top with fresh cilantro and a wedge of lime, and make sure to bitch and moan about how long this dish took so that everyone you make it for knows they now owe you one.

Serves 4

Bacon Cheddar Jalapeño Cornbread with Honey Butter

Plain old cornbread is good enough on its own, but with the addition of bacon, cheddar, jalapeño, and honey butter, it's worth ruining a marriage over. But it probably won't come to that, unless you have unresolved issues and don't communicate well; then this bacony, spicy, cheesy quinceañera of a cornbread may fill you with such happiness that you see your marriage in a new light and realize that your partner has never once, in over a decade together, made you feel this good, so you leave the bad situation you thought you could never escape, and even though it's painful and lonely at first, you rediscover yourself in a fusion of pork, carbs, and butter and make strides toward real lasting happiness, and now you don't have to share the cornbread with anyone when you make it, and suddenly it all feels worth it.

Cornbread
- 6 slices bacon, cooked and chopped into ½-inch pieces, grease reserved
- 1 cup cornmeal
- 1 cup all-purpose flour
- 1 tablespoon baking powder
- ½ teaspoon salt
- 1 stick unsalted butter, melted and cooled
- 1 cup buttermilk
- 1 egg, whisked
- 1 tablespoon honey
- 1 cup shredded sharp cheddar cheese
- 1 jalapeño, seeds removed, minced

Honey Butter
- 2 sticks unsalted butter, room temperature
- ¼ cup honey
- Kosher salt and freshly ground black pepper

Preheat your oven to 400°F. In a large heavy oven-safe skillet over medium-high heat, fry the bacon, turning occasionally until browned and wonderful, about 10 minutes. Transfer the bacon to a paper towel–lined plate, and don't you dare throw out that bacon grease. Put the skillet with the bacon grease in the oven to keep it warm.

In a large mixing bowl, combine the cornmeal, flour, baking powder, and salt. Add in the melted butter, buttermilk, egg, and honey and stir until combined. Don't overmix the batter unless you have a hankering for subpar cornbread. Mix in the chopped bacon, cheddar cheese, and jalapeño until it's evenly incorporated.

Remove the skillet from the oven and pour the batter into it. Use a spatula to smooth the surface, then put it back in the oven to bake for 20 minutes.

While it's baking, make the honey butter. Using an upright or hand mixer—or, if you don't have either of those, a whisk and some elbow grease—combine the butter and honey and whip them until smooth. Season with salt and pepper to taste.

Remove the cornbread from the oven and let it cool for 5 minutes, which, if you didn't fuck anything up, will feel like an eternity, then slice and serve with a large dollop of honey butter.

Serves 4 to 6

Romesco Sauce

This sauce makes everything it touches good. It turns bread into a meal and vegetables into something you actually want to eat, and meat and seafood are literally begging large food corporations to slaughter them en masse just so they can end up being dipped in this heavenly concoction. A warning: this recipe will feel like I'm elaborately plotting to waste 45 minutes of your time and also a bunch of random ingredients; I'll ask you to intentionally burn the shit out of the vegetables and put stale bread and nuts in a blender, and yet somehow in the end, like a mediocre white man, everything works out perfectly.

2 large red bell peppers,
   whole
1 large ripe tomato, whole
1 white onion, roughly
   chopped
4 garlic cloves, whole with
   skin on
½ cup blanched almonds
½ cup extra-virgin olive oil
3 tablespoons chopped
   fresh parsley

2 tablespoons sherry
   vinegar
1 teaspoon smoked paprika
½ teaspoon cayenne
   pepper, more if you want
   it spicy
½ cup old-ish bread torn in
   small pieces
Kosher salt and freshly
   ground black pepper

Preheat the broiler on your oven to high and line a sheet pan with aluminum foil. Add the bell peppers, tomato, onion, and garlic to the sheet pan and place it on the top rack beneath the broiler. You want to char the outside of the vegetables, not start a kitchen fire or burn them into an inedible ash, so keep an eye on things and turn them occasionally using tongs. Remove from the oven when the vegetables are charred black all over, about 10 minutes. You can also do this on a grill with the vegetables on the grates directly over the flames. The broiler is easier, but hey, it's a free country, sorta.

Let the vegetables cool for 5 minutes, then peel the skin off the peppers and remove the seeds and throw them away. Peel the outer skin from the onions and garlic cloves and discard. My God, look at you, so wasteful.

Add the charred vegetables to a blender or food processor with the almonds, oil, parsley, vinegar, paprika, cayenne pepper, and bread and purée until smooth. If the sauce is dry, add more olive oil 1 tablespoon at a time and purée until saucy. If it's wet, add a few extra chunks of bread and purée until it thickens. Taste the sauce and adjust the seasoning with salt and pepper, then serve with absolutely anything.

Makes a lot of sauce

Cajun Corn

I grew up in western New York (go Bills!), where the best barbecue by a wide margin was a place called Dinosaur Bar-B-Que, an emporium of smoked meats, cheap beers, and long soul-crushing lines of hangry people tired of being teased by the heavenly aromas wafting from the smokers. I love Dinosaur Bar-B-Que more than I love most of my relatives and 100 percent of my friends, but I do not like waiting for my food, or really anything, because I'm a control freak who you should be glad you don't have to deal with in real life. Cajun corn was one of Dinosaur's seasonal side dishes and was always my favorite, and thanks to my impatience and resourcefulness, I re-created ("stole" is such a dirty word) their recipe. While it's probably not quite as good as theirs, you can make this one in under 15 minutes and not have to have any human contact (you can even order the rub online), so really it all evens out in the end.

4 tablespoons unsalted
   butter
2 tablespoons olive oil
2 tablespoons minced garlic
4 cups corn kernels cut off
   the cob
2 tablespoons Dinosaur
   BBQ Cajun Foreplay rub,
or whatever lesser Cajun
   rub you want because you
   didn't plan ahead
3 tablespoons chopped
   fresh Italian parsley
Kosher salt and freshly
   ground black pepper

Three days before you have the idea to cook this recipe, go on the internet and buy as much Dinosaur BBQ Cajun Foreplay rub as you can afford. You won't regret it.

Put a large heavy skillet over medium-high heat and add the butter and olive oil. When the butter is completely melted, add the garlic and sauté until it just starts to brown, 30 seconds to 1 minute. If you burn the garlic, throw it out and start again. We'll wait.

Add the corn kernels to the skillet and stir to coat them in the butter and olive oil. Sauté until they start to brown and caramelize, stirring constantly, 3 to 5 minutes. Add the Cajun rub, season with plenty of salt and pepper, and cook for 2 to 4 more minutes. Taste the corn and adjust the seasonings until you start garbling in incomprehensible Cajun, then remove from the heat and stir in the fresh parsley until equally distributed.

Serves 4

The Perfect Pot of Rice

Rice is the most important food on the planet other than buffalo wings. It keeps billions of people alive, it's cheap and delicious, and if you follow my instructions, it's impossible to fuck up. There's a trick to getting the perfect ratio of rice to water, and all you need is a finger. A mangled stump will also work, in a pinch.

The Finger (or Stump) Trick:

* Put however much rice you want in the pan and set on a flat surface.

* Place the tip of your middle finger on top of the rice.

* Add water to the pan until the level reaches the line on your first knuckle. If you are using a stump, add water until the level is ¾ inch from the stump bottom.

I don't know why this trick works, but it does. Fuck measuring. Fuck ratios. Your finger (or stump) is all you need.

Rinse your rice in a fine-mesh sieve until the water runs clear. Take your time; do not rush this. It takes 1 minute, and if your time is so precious that you can't spare 1 minute, then you deserve rice covered in starchy powder that causes clumping, sticking, and failure.

Add the rice to a saucepan and set the pan on a flat surface. Place your middle finger on top of the rice and add water to the pan until the level reaches the line on your first knuckle. Add a pinch of salt and put the pan over medium-high heat until it comes to a boil, then reduce the heat to low, cover the pan with a lid, and let it cook undisturbed for 20 minutes.

Remove the pan from the heat and let the rice sit for at least 10 minutes, covered. When ready to serve, uncover it, fluff the cooked rice with a fork, and never be fearful of dying from starvation again.

Makes ∞

Apple Pistachio Crisp with Bourbon Whipped Cream

I'm not the best baker in the world, and thank you, I agree—it did take a lot of courage for me to admit that. I pathologically don't like being told what to do and will instinctively do the exact opposite of what's asked of me, because who anointed that person fucking king for a day? Making a good fruit crisp hinges on two things: the quality of the fruit and the crispiness of the crisp, so don't use bunk gas station apples, and take your time when making the crisp, and if you can't handle me telling you what to do and feel like ad-libbing, trust me: I completely understand, but don't; suck it up and follow the instructions.

Apple Crisp

- 6 tablespoons unsalted butter, divided
- 3 cups peeled and sliced Honeycrisp or Jonagold apple
- 3 cups peeled and sliced Granny Smith or other tart apple
- 1 teaspoon cinnamon, divided
- 1 teaspoon cardamom
- ½ teaspoon ground ginger
- ½ cup plus 2 tablespoons granulated sugar, divided
- Pinch of salt
- ¾ cup old-fashioned rolled oats
- ½ cup chopped pistachios

Bourbon Whipped Cream

- 1 cup heavy cream
- ¼ cup confectioners' sugar
- 1 ½ tablespoons bourbon
- Pinch of kosher salt

Preheat your oven to 375°F. Spread 1 tablespoon of butter onto a paper towel—or if you don't have to do your own laundry, a clean dish rag—and wipe it all over the inside of an 8-inch square baking pan.

In a mixing bowl, toss the sliced apples with ½ teaspoon of cinnamon, the cardamom, the ginger, 2 tablespoons of sugar, and a pinch of salt; then mix it all together until evenly coated. Dump the apples in the prepared baking pan.

To make the delicious crispy topping, add the remaining ½ teaspoon of cinnamon, ½ cup sugar, oats, pistachios, and 5 tablespoons butter to a large bowl. Using your hands, work the ingredients together, pinching the butter with your fingertips to break it up and incorporate it. You want the mixture to turn into small pea-sized lumps. If you have gargantuan boulders of crispiness, you're not done yet; keep mixing. I don't care if your fingers hurt; you're in too deep to quit now.

Spread the topping over the apple mixture and bake for about 40 minutes, until the topping is browned and your kitchen smells like what you imagine Martha Stewart's house smells like when she's going to have company over. Remove from the oven and let cool.

To make the bourbon whipped cream, use a mixer to beat the heavy cream until it starts to thicken. Add the confectioners' sugar and bourbon and beat until it starts to become all whipped cream–like, about 3 to 4 minutes. Serve the apple crisp hot with a big dollop of whipped cream and maybe a couple of pulls from the bourbon bottle. You earned it.

Serves 4 to 6

Raspberry Orange Yogurt Cake

If you suck at cooking, you're probably even worse at baking. This cake is so unfuckupable that even you can't help but make it perfectly, which will probably fill you with so much false confidence that you'll believe you're capable of anything, so please, stay grounded. Usually fresh fruit is better than frozen, but not with this cake. The freezing keeps the raspberries juicy while they bake so that they don't dry out and ruin the unruinable, thereby making you lose your last remaining shred of self-confidence and throwing you into a dangerous spiral that even a slice of cake won't pull you out of because it's dry and disgusting, and you'll look for someone else to blame, but you won't find it unless for some reason you're looking in a mirror.

½ tablespoon unsalted
   butter
1 cup full-fat plain yogurt
¾ cup granulated sugar
¼ cup vegetable oil
3 large eggs
Grated zest of 1 orange

1 cup almond flour
1 cup all-purpose flour
2 teaspoons baking powder
½ teaspoon kosher salt
1 cup frozen raspberries,
   divided

Preheat your oven to 350°F and line the bottom of a 9-inch cake pan with a round piece of parchment paper. If you don't have a 9-inch cake pan, well then, we're not off to a great start, now, are we? Find the closest pan you have in size and shape and evenly spread the ½ tablespoon of butter over the inside with a paper towel so that the cake doesn't stick.

In a large mixing bowl, add yogurt, sugar, oil, eggs, and orange zest and whisk to combine.

In a separate bowl, combine the two flours, baking powder, and salt. Combine the wet and dry ingredients and mix together just until incorporated. Don't overmix the batter, or Mary Berry will come to your house and haughtily call it "stodgy."

Scrape half of the batter into the cake pan and scatter half of the raspberries all around it; don't push the berries into the batter unless you are partial to highly unequal berry distributions in your baked goods. Pour the rest of the batter atop the berries and repeat the scattering with the other half of the berries.

Bake until the top is golden brown, about 35 minutes. If you're unsure about doneness, stick a toothpick or sharp knife into the cake. If it comes out clean, you're done; if it's gooey, bake for another 3 to 5 minutes and recheck, then repeat. Let the cake cool for 15 minutes, which I promise will be torture as the aroma taunts you. To get the cake out of the pan, put a large plate on top of the cake pan and carefully invert it to hopefully unmold it. If it sticks, just confidently declare that's what you meant to do while scraping your shame from the pan.

Makes one 9-inch cake

All the Things Cookies

Everybody should be able to make cookies, unless of course you're content suckling at the mangled diseased teat of giant food corporations that will gladly sell you overly processed chemical shit for way more money than it costs to make a batch of your own. Cookies are incredible fresh out of the oven. Their goodness then decreases linearly by the hour for a period of 72 hours, at which point they transform from heavenly dessert to flavored sand that will suffocate you with dryness, but luckily for you, these cookies won't last that long. In 30-ish minutes you will go from no dessert to fresh homemade dessert and canfinally take a bite out of the dirty profits of Big Cookie.

¾ cup unsalted butter, at
   room temperature
¾ cup granulated sugar
¾ cup light brown sugar
2 teaspoons vanilla extract
2 large eggs
2 cups all-purpose flour
1 teaspoon baking soda

½ teaspoon salt
½ cup chocolate chips
½ cup peanut butter chips
1/3 cup shredded sweetened
   coconut
1/3 cup mini pretzels, roughly
   chopped

Preheat your oven to 375°F and line two baking sheets with parchment paper.

Beat the butter until smooth using either a stand mixer with a paddle attachment, a hand mixer, or a Puerto Rican street gang armed with butterfly knives, flags, and baseball bats. In a display of racial unity, add the white and brown sugars together with the vanilla extract and beat until smooth, 1 to 2 minutes. Add the eggs one at a time and beat just until incorporated. Don't crack the eggs directly into the batter because, knowing you, you'll get eggshell in there, and if you'll please review the ingredients list one more time, you'll notice eggshells aren't on there.

In a separate bowl, whisk the flour with the baking soda and salt. Add the dry ingredients to the wet and beat just until incorporated. Don't overmix it, or an unspeakable tragedy will befall your household in the form of cakey, overly dense cookies, or your firstborn will just up and die; there's no way to tell which, and either way it's not good. Add the chocolate chips, peanut butter chips, shredded coconut, and mini pretzels and mix for 10 to 15 seconds more, just until everything is incorporated.

Divide the cookie dough into equal-sized balls on the prepared baking sheets, leaving a few inches between cookies so that they don't turn into one massive cookie that reminds you of your failures and lack of faculties. Bake for 10 to 12 minutes, until they are golden brown around the edges, then remove from the oven and cool for however long you can resist eating. My record is 3 minutes and 23 seconds.

Makes about 2 dozen cookies

Rice Krispie Treats

Everyone needs a go-to homemade dessert, and this is the easiest one on the planet. There are four ingredients total. If you can't make Rice Krispie treats, please put the book down, or better yet, get rid of it entirely because you're gonna make me look bad. Rice Krispie treats, in all their divine glory, would not be possible if not for the contributions of Dr. John Harvey Kellogg, who began experimenting with breakfast cereals as a way to encourage folks not to eat highly flavorful foods, which he deemed "sexually aggressive" and believed led to sinful masturbation. (I'm not making this up.) Dr. Kellogg would likely be rolling in his opulent grave if he learned that the masses took his boring old cereal and turned it into a gooey, delicious treat, so in his honor, please try to refrain from touching yourself for at least 30 minutes after eating.

| 6 tablespoons unsalted butter | 2 teaspoons vanilla extract |
| 1 pound mini marshmallows, divided | 6 cups Rice Krispies, or whatever cereal you feel like using |

Line a 9-inch square baking dish with parchment paper. If you don't have a 9-inch square baking dish, you're probably the exact type of sexual deviant that Dr. Kellogg warned of, so just do the best with what you've got.

Put a large saucepan over low heat and melt the butter. Add all but 1 cup of the marshmallows, stirring constantly until they're completely melted, then remove the pan from the heat.

Add the vanilla extract, whatever cereal you're using, and the remaining 1 cup of marshmallows and stir it all up until it turns into a giant, sticky, unmanageable mess that makes you begin to regret this undertaking.

Pour everything into the prepped baking dish. Using your hands, or if you don't have hands, your feet or stumps, press the mixture gently into the baking dish until it's evenly spread out. Don't press them too hard into the pan, or they will stick and you'll have to desperately dig them out of the pan with a spoon like a real-life *Cathy* cartoon. Now comes the hardest part—let the Rice Krispie treats set for 1 hour, then slice, eat, and try not to touch yourself.

Makes 10 servings

Crunchy Fucking Brownies

When I was growing up, my parents owned and operated a small children's camp in the northern foothills of the Adirondack Mountains. Our basement was littered with camping gear; dusty, patched-up cot mattresses; and first aid kits containing numerous life-saving as well as endangering supplies. I was eight when I first discovered these kits, and they provided hours of fun as I imagined I was an army medic or a doctor, but definitely not a nurse because doing more work for less pay was not my thing. EpiPens were my favorite part of the kits: spring-loaded needles that shot mystery liquid, until I accidentally injected myself in the hand with one. I instantly felt a hot wave run over me, so like a little titty-baby, I yelled for my mom. Things got tense fast. "Call 911!" Someone whisked me out of the basement and dropped me at the kitchen table. A plate of brownies was plunked down in front of me. I ate one, then another, and another, nobody paying any attention or caring about my wanton lack of portion control (and these were Jews). My parents were crying, huddled around the phone, awaiting the fate of the beloved favorite child (I lived), but all I remember is the brownies. So I guess the lesson in all this is if you are ever in a potential life-or-death emergency, make brownies, and everything will turn out okay.

1 stick plus 1 tablespoon unsalted butter, divided	2 teaspoons vanilla extract
2 cups semisweet chocolate chips	¾ cup all-purpose flour
	½ teaspoon baking powder
3 large eggs	½ teaspoon kosher salt
1 cup granulated sugar	½ cup Frosted Flakes
	½ cup hazelnuts, crushed

Preheat your oven to 350°F and line the bottom of an 8-inch square baking dish with parchment paper. Spread 1 tablespoon of butter onto a paper towel and rub it all over the pan and parchment paper to prevent the brownies from sticking, thereby minimizing any potential wasted brownie.

Add the chocolate chips and butter to a heat-proof, microwave-safe mixing bowl. Microwave for 30 seconds at a time, then remove and give it a stir and repeat until the chocolate is melted, smooth, and saucy. Set the chocolate mixture aside to cool at room temperature.

In a mixing bowl, combine the eggs, sugar, and vanilla extract and whisk until smooth and frothy. Make sure the chocolate is cool—otherwise it will curdle the eggs (not fancy)—and slowly pour it into the egg mixture. Don't overmix your batter, or I will come to your house, steal your brownies, then chastise you for their dense shittiness caused by ignoring my clearly laid-out directions.

In another mixing bowl, combine the flour, baking powder, and salt. Fold the dry ingredients into the chocolate mixture in a few batches until combined, stopping when the white flecks disappear and the batter is the color of Justin Trudeau's face on Halloween. Add the Frosted Flakes and hazelnuts and stir just until incorporated.

Scrape the batter into the baking dish and use a spatula to smooth the top so that it's evenly distributed. Bake for 25 minutes. Stick a toothpick in the center. If it comes out mostly clean, pull the brownies out of the oven because they're ready; if it comes out covered in brownie goo, bake for 5 more minutes and recheck. Let the brownies cool in the pan for 15 minutes, then cut them into however many portions you feel like, reserving a few for life-and-death emergencies.

Makes 16 brownies

Raspberry Frosé

Frosé—or frozen rosé, if you have no imagination—will give you a drinking problem in the best possible sense (and also the less good literal sense). It's the perfect drink for teenagers or sheltered adults to get drunk on for the first time in their sad lives because it doesn't taste alcoholic, so it goes down easy, at least until the ER nurse straps you to the bed and forces a corrugated plastic tube down your throat in order to pump your stomach. A word of warning: this is not a spur-of-the-moment drink; it's a plan-a-day-ahead-and-be-rewarded-for-your-delicious-foresight drink. This recipe takes time, and since hydration is of the utmost importance and gives your skin that healthy dewy look, you should probably double, triple, or quadruple the recipe, just to be safe.

1 (750 ml) bottle rosé
8 ounces raspberries, frozen
1 tablespoon honey
4 ounces vodka

8 fresh mint leaves, plus
more for garnish if you're
fancy

Pour the bottle of rosé into ice cube trays and transfer into the freezer for at least 4 hours. Through a combination of black magic and endothermic reactions, the rosé should turn into a slushy solid but won't freeze completely unless you accidentally bought alcohol-free rosé, and if you did, like, oh my God, what are you even doing?

Once the rosé is frozen-ish, add it to a blender with the frozen raspberries, honey, vodka, and mint leaves. Purée until slushy. If it's too liquidy, put the blender jar in the freezer for 30-ish minutes to thicken. When you're ready to serve, purée it for 3 to 5 seconds to break up any ice that formed, then divide among glasses and wish you quintupled the recipe.

Makes 6-ish drinks

Ginger Blackberry Bramble

Making cocktails for people is a great way to look considerate without actually having to be considerate of anyone but yourself. Cooking and baking take time and can turn out not great if you're doing it without the aid of a handsome and clever food Sherpa like yours truly. This cocktail only takes a few minutes, it's unbelievably easy, and even if you somehow do manage to screw it up, as long as you didn't forget to add the alcohol, it will still accomplish its intended goal—at least until you wake up the next morning dehydrated, disoriented, and with your mouth tasting like a cat shit in it while you slept.

5 blackberries, plus more for garnish	2 ounces vodka
1 ½-inch piece ginger, peeled, quartered	1 tablespoon lemon juice
	1 tablespoon simple syrup
	Crushed ice

First and most importantly, get a number of disparate nonsensical tattoos, dress like a steampunk clown, wear suspenders, and angrily correct anyone who dares to refer to you as a *bartender* and not your true title, *mixologist*.

Add the blackberries and ginger into a mixing glass or cocktail shaker. Use the handle of a wooden spoon or, if you're an insufferable yuppie, a cocktail muddler to smash them into a paste. Add the vodka, lemon juice, simple syrup, and some ice and shake or stir for 20 seconds. Count out loud; don't cheat.

Strain everything into a rocks glass filled with crushed ice. If you don't have crushed ice, crush it yourself. I am hopeful and perhaps foolishly optimistic that you will find a way. Discard the berries in the cocktail shaker, or better yet, eat them and get your buzz on and also valuable antioxidants and whatnot.

To finish, add some more blackberries for garnish—after all, you drink with your eyes first—then repeat until you can't remember why you started drinking in the first place.

Makes 1 drink

The Elvis

When most people hear of Elvis's cocktail, they think it's made from peanut butter, bacon, banana, a mélange of barbiturates, and topped with a splash of appropriating African American music but catering to a white audience whose inherent racial biases won't allow them to enjoy the music if performed by an African American artist. And while those may be associated with Elvis the man, they've got nothing to do with Elvis the cocktail. The Elvis is light and refreshing yet packed with booze. It's good just about anytime, anywhere, except while sitting on the toilet with opioid-induced constipation and choking on your vomit. Long live the King.

2 ounces fresh grapefruit
   juice
2 ounces London dry gin
½ ounce St-Germain or
   other elderflower liqueur

Ice
4 ounces India pale ale
1 sprig fresh mint

Combine the grapefruit juice, gin, and elderflower liqueur in whatever cocktail glass you decide to use and stir to combine. If you are a dad, please consider doing this in a cocktail shaker so you can sing "All Shook Up" as you shake (non-dads, just use a mixing glass; the joke won't work without aggressive dad energy).

Fill the glass with ice and slowly pour in the IPA. Garnish with a sprig of mint and pace yourself, unless you want a cocktail posthumously named after you.

Makes 1 drink

Watermelon Mint Frozen Margarita

Most everyone except for prudes and Mormons has a type of alcohol that causes them to writhe in pain and dry heave at the mere mention of it; for me, it's tequila. On my twenty-second birthday, a group of well-intentioned coworkers took me to some bar in Manhattan and proceeded to feed me shots of tequila blanco until I passed out. The hours following were some pretty messy time travel. First I woke up in a grocery store checkout line with a large party platter of assorted cheeses, dried meats, and crackers meant for 12 to 18 hungry guests. Then someone put me in a cab; then I somehow ended up on the subway with the party platter. Not being the type to waste food, I tried to quash my drunkenness by consuming the roughly seven and a half pounds of party platter, until I spontaneously emptied my stomach, as well as an entire subway car of people, in a violent expulsion of neon cheese, tastefully aged meats, and tequila. It took me almost a decade to face tequila again, and when I did, it was in this drink, which is so fruity that you'll forget there's alcohol in it, at least until you drink a couple too many and wake up in an ice bath in Mexico; then you'll probably piece it together.

1 tablespoon kosher salt	1 cup tequila blanco
1 lime wedge	½ cup triple sec
2 cups watermelon cut into	½ cup lime juice
1-inch cubes	2 tablespoons simple syrup
10 sprigs fresh mint	6 cups ice

Salt the rim of your glass to start; if you hate salty rims, then first of all, how dare you? And second of all, skip this step. Pour the salt onto a small plate. Rub the rim of whatever glass you're using with a wedge of lime, then dip the rim in the salt until it's coated. Set aside.

In a blender, combine the watermelon, mint, tequila blanco, triple sec, lime juice, simple syrup, and ice. Blend until smooth, about 30 seconds. Pour the mixture into the salt-rimmed glass (or non-salt-rimmed glass if you're not a rimmer) and top with ice.

Makes 2 to 4 drinks

Index